THE AUTHOR

The Hermetic Art

AN INTRODUCTION TO
THE ART OF ALCHEMY

The Text of the Hermetic Sermons, Entitled, "The Greatest Ill Among Men Is Ignorance of God," "That No One of Existing Things Doth Perish," and the Sermon on Thought and Sense, Together With the Esoteric Commentary, Giving in Full, the Esoteric Key to These Three Great Sermons, The Official Interpretation of the Hermetic Brotherhood of Atlantis, and the Official Text Book in the Hermetic Art.

By

DR. A. S. RALEIGH

THE
HERMETIC PUBLISHING COMPANY
3006 Lake Park Avenue, Chicago, Ill.
1919

Type Set by American Typesetting Corporation, Chicago
Printed and Bound by M. A. Donohue & Co., Chicago

DEDICATION

To that small but select body of students
of Alchemy scattered throughout the
world—who have ever devoted themselves to the Quest after the Absolute,
and have sought for the Philosopher's
Stone—this course of Lessons in the Hermetic Art is lovingly dedicated, with the
hope that it may in some degree throw
light upon the subject of their search, and
may to some extent direct them in the way
of the real Transmutation.

THE AUTHOR.

CONTENTS.

INTRODUCTORY NOTE

In presenting this series of lessons on the Hermetic Art we are continuing the series which began in Philosophia Hermetica, which continued in Scientific Hermetica and culminated in the Hermetic Art, this series of three books being intended as an introduction to the study of alchemy. In the Philosophia Hermetica we gave an introduction to the Philosophy of Alchemy, in Scientific Hermetica we gave an introduction to the Science of Alchemy and in the Hermetic Art we give an introduction to the Art of Alchemy. All Hermetic matters group themselves under those three heads. Hermetic Philosophy, which deals with the speculative side of Hermeticism, Hermetic Science which deals with the scientific principles embodied in the Hermetic teaching and the Hermetic Art which deals with the practical application of the principles enunciated in the Hermetic Philosophy and the Hermetic Science. Physical alchemy is by the novice generally supposed to be the summum bonum of Hermeticism, while as a matter of fact it is a very unimportant item in the general body of our teaching. The basis of Hermeticism as we have it today is to be found in the writing of Hermes Trismegistus. In all those writings there is not a single sermon devoted to the discussion of practical alchemy, and yet there are those so damnably ignorant as to assume that Hermeticism is primarily concerned with the physical side of the Magnum Opus. To those who hold this view we can only reply that Hermeticism is a complete philosophy of life, it represents absolute truth. It begins with religion, it is essentially a system of theology, it has next its metaphysical side, closely connected with the theological element; it is philosophical, it is also metaphysical, it has its peculiar psychology. It is related to the whole body of the Kosmos and all that proceeds from it, which of course includes Alchemy. But Alchemy is merely one of the sciences which Hermes Trismegistus was very careful to point out should not be confounded with philosophy and Hermes announced himself to be a teacher of philosophy primarily. His discussion of the sciences was merely incidental to his work of propounding philosophical religion. T h e Metaphysics of Alchemy always precedes the Physics of Alchemy even when we come to discuss the alchemical aspect of the Hermetic Art. Therefore in the succeeding course of lessons which will immediately follow these we propose to discuss the Philosophy of Alchemy, this will be followed by a course in the Science of Alchemy, this in turn by one in the Speculative Art of Alchemy and the seventh volume of the series will be the first to deal with the Practical Art of Alchemy.

It may be said that one cannot consummate Practical Alchemy until one has first understood Kosmical Alchemy,—that is to say the Alchemy which is perpetually going on in Kosmos. After this he must understand Mental Alchemy, or the Alchemy operating within the mind through which thoughts are generated and through which thought is transmuted, then he must understand the Alchemy of the soul and after these the Alchemy of the physical body. Furthermore he must have accomplished the Alchemy of his own mind, soul and body before he can accomplish the Physical Alchemy which is related to the transmutation of metals; therefore it is necessary to understand the Metaphysics of Alchemy before one attempts to concentrate his attention on the physical aspect of practical alchemy.

This work is not only to be viewed in the sense of a treatise on the Hermetic Art and an intro-

duction to the Philosophy of Alchemy, it is in fact
the official text book of the Hermetic Brotherhood
on that subject. There have been a great many
works on Alchemy written by those who knew
absolutely nothing of what they were talking
about, but in our Hermetic Art we are giving you
the official authorized text book of the Brotherhood dealing with the Hermetic Art, and likewise their official authorized introduction to the
study of the Philosophy of Alchemy, but in addi-
tion to this the book will also be found to contain
the text of three of the sermons of Hermes Trismegistus together with the official commentary
unfolding their Esoteric meaning. These sermons are the ones entitled, "The Greatest Ill
Among Men Is Ignorance of God, That no one of
existing things doth perish but men in error speak
of their changes as destructions and as deaths, and
the sermon on Thought and Sense, That the beau-
tiful and the good is in God only and elsewhere
nowhere." Those who do not desire to study the
Hermetic Art or to enter into the study of Alchemy
will nevertheless find the lessons interesting as
they constitute the official and authoritative commentary on these three sermons. One should not
attempt to read the future books on Alchemy without thoroughly mastering the contents of Philosophia Hermetica, Scientific Hermetica and the
Hermetic Art. We present this effort to our read-
ers and friends with the hope that it may interest
them to look more deeply into the rich mine of
occult, mystic and philosophical lore which is contained in the writings of Thrice Greatest Hermes.
In giving forth this book we feel that we have dis-
charged an obligation which rested upon us to give
to the world the absolute truth in regard to the
three heads of Hermetic teaching, Philosophia
Hermetica, Scientific Hermetica and the Hermetic
Art. In doing this we have placed all without

excuse, who fall for the mediocre unofficial publications that are put forth from time to time by novices who know absolutely nothing of what they are writing. By giving this official information we have provided the world with the standard text books of the three heads of Hermetic knowledge. It is to be hoped that they will make good use of them, at any rate they are provided with accurate information in regard to the subject.

With the publication of this volume we will have provided students with a complete introduction to all departments of the Hermetic Gnosis. This was the work which we assigned ourselves in the beginning and having accomplished the task we have now equipped the reader with all the preliminary instructions which he requires for boldly entering into the study of alchemy. It is to be trusted that those who have understood our teaching will have the boldness to go into this field of *Creative work*.

A. S. RALEIGH.

Columbus, Ohio, July 1, 1916.

The Hermetic Art

The Greatest Ill Among Men Is Ignorance of God

TEXT

Parthey (G.), *Hermetic Trismegisti Poemander* (Berlin, 1854), 54-55.

Patrizzi (F.), *Nova de Universis Philosophia* (Venice, 1593), 18a.

Mead (G. R. S.), *Thrice Greatest Hermes* (London, 1906), Corpus Hermeticum VII (VIII).

1. Whither stumble ye, sots, who have sopped up the wine of ignorance unmixed, and can so far not carry it that ye already even spew it forth?

Stay ye, be sober, gaze upwards with the [true] eyes of the heart! And if ye cannot all, yet ye at least who can!

For that the ill of ignorance doth pour o'er all the earth and overwhelm the soul that's battened down within the body, preventing it from fetching port within Salvation's harbours.

2. Be then not carried off by the fierce flood, but using the shore-current, ye who can, make for Salvation's port, and, harbouring there, seek ye for one to take you by the hand and lead you unto, Gnosis' gates.

Where shines clear Light, of every dark-ness clean; where not a single soul is drunk, but sober all they gaze with their heart's eyes on Him who willeth to be seen.

No ear can hear Him, nor can eye see Him, nor tongue speak of Him, but [only] mind and heart.

But first thou must tear off from thee the cloak which thou dost wear,—the web of ignorance, the ground of bad, corruption's chain, the carapace of darkness, the living death, sensation's corpse, the tomb thou car-riest with thee, the robber in thy house, who through the things he loveth, hateth thee, and through the things he hateth, bears thee malice.

3.   Such is the hateful cloak thou wear-est,—that throttles thee [and holds thee] down to it, in order that thou may'st not gaze above, and, having seen the Beauty of the Truth, and Good that dwells therein, detest the bad of it; having found out the plot that it hath schemed against thee, by making void of sense those seeming things which men think senses.

For that it hath with mass of matter blocked them up and crammed them full of loathsome lust, so that thou may'st not hear about the things that thou should'st hear, nor see the things that thou should'st see.

LESSON I

The Ill of Ignorance

1. Wither stumble ye, sots, who have sopped up the wine of ignorance unmixed, and can so far not carry it that ye already even spew it forth?

Stay ye, be sober, gaze upwards with the [true] eyes of the heart! And if ye cannot all, yet ye at least who can!

For that the ill of ignorance doth pour o'er all the earth and overwhelm the soul that's battened down within the body, preventing it from fetching port within Salvation's harbors.

This sermon is in the nature of an impassioned appeal to the people to refrain from the drunkenness of ignorance and turn their attention to the truth. It is in the nature of a preaching an evangelical preachment of the beauty of Gnosis versus the ugliness and degradation of the life of the senses. In order to make the lesson the more impressive he compares the people to sots who are continually in a state of intoxication, who stumble through life dependent entirely on the testimony of their senses for guidance. It is very graphically expressed. He begins by inquiring Whither stumble ye? In other words, they are described as stumbling through life in a state of intoxication. He terms them sots, and asserts they have sopped up the wine of ignorance unmixed. Ignorance is here compared to a steady diet of wine, because the effect of ignorance is to produce a state of mental and spiritual intoxication very similar to

13

the state of intoxication produced by over-indulgence in wine. Ignorance is thus viewed as a positive intoxicant; a poison having the effect of clouding the mind so that it is incapable of thinking clearly. He states that this wine of ignorance is unmixed. That is to say there is not a particle of truth in what they are imbibing. There being no mixture of truth in the wine of ignorance their souls are entirely dominated by the intoxication growing out of this unmixed wine of ignorance. He further says that they can so far not carry it, that they already even spew it forth. In other words the mind, saturated by the wine of ignorance is incapable of retaining its own supply of ignorance but spews it forth similar to the drunkard spewing forth the overabundance of wine which he has taken. By this he means that the ignorance intoxicated man gives expression to no thought, word or deed but what springs directly from ignorance. In other words, no good, true or logical statement can ever by any possibility emanate from the consciousness of one intoxicated by ignorance. His statements will all be untrue, his deeds will all be evil, his thoughts will all be irrational. He leads a life expressive of pure and unadulterated ignorance, because all his thinking has been inspired by ignorance. We must understand this matter in its true light; that is to say, we must get a true understanding of his usage of the term ignorance.

Hermes, being a metaphysician and a transcendentalist, takes the common position of all such philosophers, that the senses always lead one astray; that our facts are all of them absolutely untrue; that the testimony of the senses is invariably misleading; consequently any view that springs from the testimony of the senses will be in the very nature of things misleading. As long as one's thinking is in terms of sense perception he will gain an erroneous view of the universe, of life, of experience, of the whole cosmogony of being. This false view of the nature of things is what he terms ignorance. It is viewed as a positive force because of the positive effect which it has upon the soul. So long as one's thinking is in terms of the senses, that is, so long as this ignorance or illusion binds ones thinking, he will be in a state of intoxication, seeing that it will be utterly impossible for him ever to think correctly, that is in accordance with the truth; because this ignorance induced by the senses, this false mental attitude, precludes the possibility of logical, rational thinking and one is intoxicated by it. His mind is deceived by the false images which his senses present to it. So that the mind, being clouded and befuddled in this way, causes him to speak and act in a false and illogical manner. Therefore the question is, Whither stumble ye? In other words, in what direction is your drunken stumbling leading you? It is very much in the nature of a rebuke to a drunkard when we put it in the form of a question and ask him where this continual drunkenness is going to lead him. It is as though to ask the drunkard where he expected to get off at if he kept it up. It is this form of interrogative rebuke that is administered. The question is, what will be the goal of anyone who continues in this state of intoxication, being continually made drunk by ignorance without receiving the light of truth.

Next he admonishes them to stay, to be sober, to gaze upwards with the true eyes of the heart. Having indicated the evil tendency of their drunkenness, which simply means a state of consciousness induced by the testimony of the senses, he next admonishes them to halt in this course of degeneracy, to stop and consider, to reckon with themselves. He admonishes them to be sober. Now as drunkenness is a condition resulting from the sopping up of the wine of ignorance sobriety of course can consist only in abstaining from imbibing the wine of ignorance. The wine of ignorance being the term used to indicate that state of mind growing out of the testimony of the senses, it follows that sobriety can only mean the discarding or rejection of the testimony of the senses and a state of consciousness growing out of the exercise of the Pure Reason independent of all sense perception. This Pure Reason will therefore enlighten the understanding, purging out the mind of ignorance induced by the testimony of the senses, and hence will develop a balanced rational state of mind which he describes as sober. Next he admonishes them to gaze upwards with the true eyes of the heart. In other words, he is clearly enunciating the doctrine of the heart versus the doctrine of the eyes. The heart is used here with reference to the devotional side of ones being working in conjunction with the Reason, the Gnostic heart in other words. The eyes of the heart refer to the soul sense, to that sense which is not discernible through the physical senses but is rather a faculty of the soul; something closely united to intuition but yet somewhat different. And then admonishes them to gaze upward, that this soul sense can, through this, come in contact with reality instead of the illusion of the senses. This attitude of contact with reality through the testimony of the Reason, the eyes of the heart, produces the sober mind rather than the intoxication of ignorance, and in this way ignorance is purged out of the soul. Realizing that it is impossible for all mankind to heed his advice, that some souls are so undeveloped that they can only feed upon ignorance, and in fact that ignorance gives them an opportunity for evolution which they would not otherwise have, seeing that they can thrive on no other diet, he does not try to persuade all to abstain from ignorance,

and the drunkenness which it induces, but calls
upon all who have the capacity to do this, all who
are able to at least follow his advice and look
upwards. Hence it is to be observed that the
Hermetic message is not directed to the multitude
but rather to those scattered within the multitude
who are capable of grasping a thought of the
higher life.

For that the ill of ignorance doth pour
o'er all the earth and overwhelm the soul
that's battened down within the body, preventing it from fetching port within Salvation's harbors.

The ill of ignorance relates to the consequences
or effects of ignorance, the evil growing out of it,
and also to ignorance itself as an ill. It is stated
that this pours o'er all the earth. In other words,
there is nothing in the sensible world but what con-
tributes to the development of this ill of ignorance.
In other words, all objects of the senses engender
sensations which in turn produce ignorance in the
human mind. Therefore the earth is completely
covered with this ill of ignorance inasmuch as all
objects in the world directly induce ignorance in
the human consciousness. It overwhelms the soul
that's battened down within the body. That is to
say all souls resident in the body, all incarnate
souls, are influenced by this ill of ignorance because
their corporeal senses are controlled and dominated by the objects of sense. These senses cause
distorted images of those objects to be reflected in
the mind in terms of corresponding mental impressions. Therefore all souls resident within the body
are influenced by the testimony of the senses so that
the soul is overwhelmed by this force of ignorance,
is controlled by it, and is unable to express itself
against this force of the obvious. It is this over-

whelming of the soul by ignorance that prevents it from fetching port within Salvation's harbors. In other words, the soul is described as a vessel at sea. Tossed about upon the waves of ignorance Salvation is the harbor to which it is bound, but it is unable to fetch port within the harbors of Salvation because it is overwhelmed by ignorance due to its residence in the body. He therefore very clearly indicates what he means by salvation. Inasmuch as ignorance induced by sense perception is that which keeps the soul from reaching salvation, it follows that salvation is the state resulting from a repudiation of the testimony of the senses. In other words, in order to reach Salvation the soul must through Reason rise above the testimony of the senses, must break away from the ideal world of sense induced thought and reach a consciousness of reality. In other words, Salvation is the state of mind growing out of knowledge of the truth rather than the facts indicated by the senses. So long, therefore, as anyone takes the testimony of his senses seriously, or gives credit to the thoughts induced by the senses Salvation is impossible. It therefore follows that Salvation is a state of consciousness directly the reverse of the ordinary human consciousness, the consciousness growing out of the testimony of the senses. It is an ideal consciousness rather than a sensible consciousness, or a sensuous consciousness, that is termed Salvation. The whole preaching of our sermon is an exhortation to strive to overcome the testimony of the senses, though abiding within the body, and reach the pure plane of truth.

2. Be then not carried off by the fierce flood, but using the shore-current, ye who can, make for Salvation's port, and, harboring there, seek ye for one to take you by the hand and lead unto Gnosis' gates.

Where shines clear light, of every darkness clean; where not a single soul is drunk, but sober all they gaze with their heart's eyes on Him who willeth to be seen.

Where no ear can hear him, nor can eye see him, nor tongue speak of him, but [only] mind and heart.

But first thou must tear off from thee the cloak which thou dost wear,—the web of ignorance, the ground of bad, Corruption's chain, the carapace of darkness, the living death, sensation's corpse, the tomb thou carriest with thee, the robber in thy house, who through the things he loveth, hateth thee, and through the things he hateth, bears thee malice.

Be then not carried off by the fierce flood, but using the shore-current, ye who can, make for Salvation's port, and, harboring there, seek ye for one to take you by the hand and lead you into Gnosis' gates.

Here he describes the force of ignorance as a fierce flood, that is as a swift flowing stream, the main current of a stream, which carries one out to sea, as it were, leading him entirely away from the true reason and consciousness of things. A current against which no one can pull. Nevertheless he urges those to whom he appeals to not be carried off by this fierce flood but overcome it, and he assures them that it is possible to do this by using the shore-current. That is to say, the back or up-current which is caused by the swift flowing of the current; the back current being induced, and which tends to flow upstream near the shore.

The advice therefore is to struggle to get out of the swift current and bring one's bark within the back or shore current, so that one may drift to shore. In this way it is possible to make for Salvation's port. The imagery here is very graphic, and yet it does not appear to be so very difficult to understand. He describes the life of sense induced thought, that is the life naturally growing out of one's mode of thinking, when that mode of thinking is induced by the testimony of the senses. This mode of life is likened to being adrift in the current of a swift flowing stream. Nevertheless from that there is a shore current which leads one away from the testimony of the senses, and this shore current is nothing more nor less than the faculty of analytical reasoning. Using the shore current means nothing more nor less than exercising ones faculty for analysis,—striving to get back of appearances and come in contact with reality. Salvation's port is the landing place from the river of ignorance, hence it relates to that stage of one's consciousness where a basis for clear thinking has been realized, where one begins to develop a philosophical concept entirely independent of the testimony of the senses. In other words, Salvation's port is the metaphysical concept. When one has reached that stage where he thinks from the metaphysical rather than from the sensory, or obvious, or physical standpoint he has entered Salvation's port.

The next instruction is to harbor there. By entering the port and harboring there he means to live temporarily in this metaphysical port, this port of the metaphysical view of life. In other words, to continue to study and contemplate life from the metaphysical point of view. Next, seek for one to take you by the hand and lead you into Gnosis' gates. He takes the position that to change one's views of life from that induced by the senses to the metaphysical, and to maintain that metaphysical view of life, is about as far as one can go by his own effort. In other words, Hermes was not a believer in the idea that one could look within and find the truth. He does not believe that it was advisable for anyone to try to attain the Gnosis by development dependent upon himself. He did not consider that there was any inner voice that could lead one to the consciousness of truth, but rather held that the metaphysical view of things was about as far as one could go without assistance. When one had reached this stage Hermes advised him to seek for an Initiate who understood the higher teachings, who understood the nature of things to a great extent, who would lead him into the gates of Gnosis. Mind you, he does not say, who would give him Gnosis, for no teacher can impart Gnosis to any human being. All the teacher can do is to teach philosophy from the standpoint of the Reason through analysis, to bring one's soul to that stage of development where he is able to reach the gates of Gnosis. Hence he advised everyone who had entered Salvation's port to remain in that state of mind, not striving to go beyond it until he had found a Master who was able through teaching to prepare him for Gnosis.

Where shines clear Light, of every darkness clean; where not a single soul is drunk, but sober all they gaze with their heart's eyes on Him who willeth to be seen.

In this paragraph we have a description of the Gnosis. In the first place, there shines clear Light. By this he does not mean physical light, nor yet cosmic light, but rather does he mean that divine ray of light from which mind proceeds. And this clear Divine Light shines in the place of Gnosis.

Within the gates of Gnosis. It is one of the conditions precedent to the attainment of Gnosis. This Light is clean of every darkness, for here in this Light there is nothing but the pure undivided Divine Light which shines into the soul of the aspirant illuminating his consciousness with this clear Divine Light. Where not a single soul is drunk, for the simple reason that this Light dispels all darkness, all ignorance, causing the light to reflect the perfect truth and thus leaving no space for ignorance. The soul being clearly illumined by the Divine Light is not drunk but sober. All souls bathed in this Light must be free of ignorance, and therefore in a state of soberness resulting from the clear consciousness of truth. So that all gaze with their heart's eyes; that is with the perception of their souls, with their soul sense, on Him who willeth to be seen, that is upon the Absolute, unmanifest God. The soul sense of the Gnosis is therefore able to give him a clear view of the unmanifest God, the God beyond all name. He it is who is the subject of their contemplation.

Where no ear can hear Him, nor can eye see Him, nor tongue speak of Him, but [only] mind and heart.

God cannot be approached through the medium of the senses, He cannot be heard, neither can He be seen, neither can He be described by words of speech. God is therefore entirely removed from the plane of the senses. He can only be seen, heard and spoken of by mind and heart. That is to say, only through intelligence and devotion is it possible for one to deal with God. Language cannot describe Him, we can only think of Him, and the heart's devotion can alone grasp His nature. Therefore God must be worshiped in thought and the devotion of the heart. Hence the Gnostic must be one whose mind is capable of thinking independently of the testimony of the senses. It must work entirely apart from the senses, dealing in the problem from altogether a different angle. In other words, it is a pure, metaphysical, mystical contemplation of mind and heart directed unto the consideration of the nature of God. The training one receives from the Master is in reality to develop this faculty of which we are speaking, the faculty for the independent operation of the mind and heart when entirely divested of the testimony of the senses.

But first thou must tear off from thee the cloak which thou dost wear,—the web of ignorance, the ground of bad, corruption's chain, the carapace of darkness, the living death, sensation's corpse, the tomb thou carriest with thee, the robber in thy house, who through the things he loveth, hateth thee, and through the things he hateth, bears thee malice.

In this paragraph he denounces the body, and announces that before one can reach this gnostic state he must tear off from him the cloak which he wears. This cloak which is worn by the soul is the body. First of all he denounces it as the web of ignorance, because of the fact that it communicates nothing true to the soul, it lies about everything—that is the physical senses misrepresent things. Next, it is the ground of bad, for nothing good can be expressed in the physical body. It is the ground of bad. We do all things because of the process of generation which goes on in the production of the body, we do all things because we have physical bodies. It is utterly impossible for the good to grow out of the physical.

Next, corruption's chain, that is to say the chain
of corruption by which we are bound. The continual process of corruption which goes on because
of the presence of the body. The carapace of
darkness, because the bodily senses shut out the
light, causing us to be guided by false testimony,
by false sensations. Thus the body shuts out the
light and binds us to darkness. The living death,
because the body going through the process of corruption, of transition, continually dies. Our life
is but a sequence of deaths. Sensation's corpse,
that is the corpse through which the senses operate, the corpse produced by sensation. Every man
is really dead so long as he is governed by the
senses. He only lives when they are overcome.
The tomb thou carriest with thee. The body is
described as the tomb in which the soul is buried.
The robber in thy house. The body and its
physical sensations rob one of the soul's life,
because so long as the corporeal and sensuous life
is led it is utterly impossible to lead the spiritual
life. Who through the things he loveth, hateth
thee. Remember the one addressed here is the
soul always, and the body, through the things it
loves, hates the soul, because it strives after physical gratification and thus prevents the spiritual
gratification of the soul. And through the things
he hateth, bears thee malice. In other words, all
the antipathies of the body are malicious because
of the attitude which they have upon the soul.

While this paragraph deals with the body as the
subject of its denunciation, the bodily life, yet there
is a secondary meaning. It is not merely the body
that is here used in its physical senses but we have
also a sort of mystical body of sensation that we
have to take into consideration, and that is perhaps
the more important of the two. Because he states
that first we must tear off the cloak which we wear
before we can enter the gates of Gnosis. Now if

this related only to the physical body it would mean that no one could attain Gnosis until he died, but the whole tenor of Hermetic teaching is the urging of people to attain Gnosis while they are yet alive. Therefore this cannot refer so much to the physical body as to a sort of mystical body of sensation, which will really mean the cloak that he speaks of here. In this sense the web of ignorance would relate to a web woven by ignorant thinking, which binds the mind as in a spider's web, so to speak; a pall, a curtain, that incloses the mind and soul, preventing them from seeing beyond it. This must be torn off first,—the web of ignorance—and we must destroy the web of ignorance by destroying ignorance with knowledge. The ground of bad, that is, the foundation from which bad proceeds. As bad is the result of genesis it will follow that to tear away the ground of bad will mean to cause the fruit of ignorance to be no longer borne. That is to prevent our previous ignorant thinking from bringing forth fruit, from generating offspring in the form of consciousness and deed. Corruption's chain must also be torn off, that is to say the sequence of corruption which is operating within our being, this must be torn away by entirely separating in our consciousness the soul life from the bodily life. No one can escape the chain of corruption so long as he looks upon the physical body as being himself. The self must be identified with the soul, and when the soul has been identified as the self, the body being no longer recognized as an integral part of the self, corruption's chain will cease to affect the soul. In other words, we must cease to believe in corruption and death and assert our immortality, and in this way corruption's chain is torn off. We must tear off the carapace of darkness. We must refuse to dwell in the dark. We must open our souls to the shining of the light, thus escaping the shell of darkness induced by ignorance and carnality of mind. The living death must be torn away by consciously living not in time but in eternity, by realizing the eternity of the soul's nature. We must cease to function in sensation's corpse by repudiating the testimony of the senses; by thinking not in terms of sense perception or experience, but in terms of the Pure Reason. No one can escape the corpse of sensation so long as he believes in the testimony of his senses. By repudiating the testimony of the senses, by refusing to accept it as true, by thinking rather in terms of eternal truth through the Pure Reason of the soul, one is able to cast aside sensation's corpse and live the spiritual life while still in the body. The tomb thou carriest with thee, is nothing more nor less than the life which one leads, his consciousness being bounded by the testimony of the senses. This leads to a belief in death and the belief in death entombs the soul in mortality, consequently the soul abiding in this mortal tomb, is shut off from the true life. The robber in thy house, is this belief in mortality induced by sensation, in other words, the mental attitude which sensation induces—such mental attitude robs the soul of its true life, in that it renders it impossible for the soul to be conscious of its true attributes seeing that the human consciousness is made up entirely of dying things, of the changes and transitions which the objects of sense indicate. This robber in the house which we have thus indicated hates the soul through the very things he loves. That is to say, as long as the consciousness is made up of the testimony of the senses, of ignorance, it will be antagonistic to every aspect of the true soul life, being entirely against the life of the soul, completely destroying whatever of the soul life tends to manifest itself, and these antipathies, that is the antipathies of the senses, befog the mind and are really antipathetic to the life of the soul. Whatever the sense induced consciousness opposes is in reality a true attribute of the soul life; therefore we are able to see that the cloak here spoken of is not only the physical body but is a sort of subjective body growing out of the direct action of the senses, a body of illusion, a body of ignorance, which must be overcome by the mind freeing itself from the illusions of the senses, and that until this has been consummated it is utterly impossible for the first gleam of Gnosis to enter the consciousness. Hence to tear off this cloak while yet in the body means that the soul must become entirely independent of all influences exercised by the body. The soul must become the positive pole and the body merely the expression on the physical plane of the soul life. So long as the body is the vehicle for the physical plane, it is the cloak of ignorance. It only ceases to be this when it becomes the vehicle for the soul operating upon the physical plane, but is in no sense influenced by the physical plane. Only in this way is one freed from the cloak of ignorance and enabled to enter the gnostic path. The path of true enlightenment. Such an one is in fact a spirit rather than a body. He is just as much a freed spirit as he is when he permanently leaves the body.

LESSON II

The Limitations of the Body

3. Such is the hateful cloak thou wearest,—that throttles thee [and holds thee] down to it, in order that thou mayst not gaze above, and, having seen the Beauty of the Truth, and Good, that dwells therein, detest the bad of it; having found out the plot that it has schemed against thee, by making void of sense those seeming things which men think senses.

For that it hath with mass of matter blocked them up and crammed them full of loathsome lust, so that thou mayst not hear about the things that thou shouldst hear, nor see the things that thou shouldst see.

In order to understand this it must be thoroughly borne in mind that the soul and body are clearly differentiated the one from the other. The soul, in the Hermetic writing, is always spoken of as the personality, the body is something separate and distinct that is made use of by the soul during its incarnate life and at the same time greatly hampers the life of the soul. Therefore the "thou" spoken of here does not include the body but represents the soul as separate and distinct from the body. This soul, however, is not to be conceived of as an impersonal ego but rather as the true personality; therefore he speaks of the body as the hateful cloak thou wearest. That is to say not only the physical body but to a certain extent the false personality induced by the body. The body and everything springing from it are described as

29

a hateful cloak. This cloak, the body and its false
personality, throttle the soul and holds it down to
it, the body, thus preventing the soul from realizing its own true life, compelling it to function
physically, forcing it to realize a purely physical
life only, and thus preventing it from gazing above
and seeing the Beauty and Truth and Good that
dwells in the realm above, preventing the soul from
detesting the bad of the lower life and preventing
it from finding out the plot that the body has
schemed against the soul by making void of sense
those seeming things which men think sense so
that one is unable to rise above this limitation of
the body. This is the real crux of the situation;
the fact that the senses are in reality void of sense;
what the senses indicate in reality—containing the
true sense. To understand this doctrine one must
bear in mind the doctrine of Kosmic Sense as
enunciated by Hermes. This doctrine of Kosmic
Sense holds to the view that there is in nature, or
in Kosmos, a principle which is termed Kosmic
Sense, and which is really the depositary of all
things sensible; that in a certain sense Kosmos is
through certain senses made aware of the existence
of all things sensible, and in fact that the sensibles
are the direct product of the Kosmic sense. To
understand this more accurately we must bear in
mind that the sensibles are the product of a creative force. Now Hermes teaches that the Kosmos
is not only endowed with thought but also with
sense, and that it is the perceptive faculty of the
Kosmos that produces the sensibles. In other
words, Kosmic sense, far from being a Kosmic faculty for the perception of things already existent,
is rather that sense which enables Kosmic thought
to become visible to the Kosmos, a sort of imaging or visualizing faculty with which Kosmos is
endowed; this visualizing or imaging faculty
enabling Kosmos to give form to its thought, thus

causing Kosmic thoughts to manifest corresponding images, which in this way, through such imaging or visualizing of Kosmis, become definite forms. In this way are all things brought into being through Kosmic sense. Thus all sensibles are created by sense. Now the theory here taken is, that it is only those things perceived into existence by Kosmic sense that really are, and that really possess sense. The things which men call sense are in reality void of sense in this Kosmic sense of the term. The reason is, this Kosmic sense brings into manifestation the things that are, while the senses of man give to him distorted images, caricatures or pictures of those things, which images or pictures are never accurate. What he pleads for is that soul sense which, when developed, will enable man to unite this sense of his with Kosmic sense and thereby sense the things as they are instead of things as they seem. A sense that will enable one to grasp noumena instead of phenomena. His indictment against the body is, in reality that the bodily senses by presenting distorted images of things prevent one from seeing the things as they are; therefore by giving a man a false sense they prevent him from attaining the true sense. Therefore he accuses the body of scheming a plot against man to deceive him, and we are only able to discover this plot when through the awakening of the true sense we have made void of sense those seeming things which men think senses, that is to say by discovering that the testimony of the senses is in reality void of true sense. Our common sense is therefore seen to be utterly senseless, because common sense is that attitude of mind which grows out of the testimony of the senses and out of all the experiences which we derive through them. This being the case it will follow that common sense will be as erroneous as the testimony of the senses, through which it is derived. In other words, common sense is at all times absolutely void of sense. In order therefore for one to see the Beauty of the Truth and Good that dwells in the realm of the soul, one must attain the true sense, and this attainment of the true sense is the all important problem with which we have to deal. But it must be borne in mind that the body's senses stand absolutely in the way, and he is indicating here the great difficulty with which we have to deal if we would attain true sense while living in the body, because the body's senses are diametrically opposed to the attainment of true sense.

For that it hath with mass of matter blocked them up and crammed them full of loathsome lust, so that thou may'st not hear about the things that thou should'st hear, nor see the things that thou should'st see.

We now come to consider the cause back of the irregularity and irresponsibility of the senses, and it is stated that that is because the senses have been blocked up with mass of matter and have been crammed full of loathsome lust. The first statement indicates the real cause,—they have been blocked up with mass of matter. And of course he is here aluding to the physical body and its massive material character. In order to understand this we must bear in mind that all sensation and all impressions of every description are due to vibration, and that vibration accomplishes its work by reason of the resistance which is offered to it, but at the same time, by reason of its ability to overcome such resistance. The rate of vibration will therefore determine the quality of such impressions. All sensation is the result of such impression growing out of vibration. Now it will follow that the more gross the matter is through which vibration moves the less rapid will be the rate of vibration which can possibly move through such matter, hence it will follow that the vibration emanating from the body, or set in motion in the ether by such body, will not be able to freely express itself through any medium more gross in its atomic and molecular structures than is the ether itself. All vibratory waves, even of a physical nature, passing through the ether, will take on the etheric vibration, consequently should they contact a body more gross than the ether their vibration will be lowered in accordance with the degree of such grossness, therefore no vibration that passes through the body as a medium, can possibly represent in sensation a condition less gross than the body. The result will be the images which are indicated to consciousness through the medium of sensation will be images distorted by the grossness of the body. It at once becomes evident that the sensations which we can possibly receive in the body must be very different from those objects which originally produced those sensations. In order to get an understanding of this difference, take into consideration the electric light, which is produced by a current of electricity passing through a filament of carbon, then imagine this same current having to pass through an iron bar an inch in diameter, and you can have some faint idea of the difference that the body makes between the original vibratory force and the sensation which we get from it. Therefore it will follow that the mass of matter through which vibration has to pass in order to awaken physical sensation is such that those sensations will never be reliable.

Next we have the statement that the body has crammed the senses full of loathsome lust. This is an outgrowth of the mass of matter that fills the senses. The loathsome lust, or desires that the senses are full of, is the result of this material cramming, because all vibration has to pass through this gross massive matter, and its form is correspondingly changed. It follows that these vibratory attractions which result from vibration, must completely change their form. The gentle attraction which would exist between rapidly moving forces has become altogether different. The result is our desires cease to be mere attractions growing out of chemical affinity and become in every sense of the term corporeal, being influenced by the sensation of form, consequently sensation must naturally express itself in the form of loathsome lust. Lust is hence nothing more than the inevitable consequence of vibratory attraction operating through the gross physical body; hence we have lust because we have bodies, and, ordinarily speaking, the body is the antecedent of lust as lust is the legitimate consequence of the body. We have thus a false personality induced by those distorted sensations and by the lust which they engender. This false personality which is the avenue through which the average man feeds his mind through which all consciousness is evolved, being made up of distorted sensations and loathsome lust, keeps the soul in bond so that the soul can only grow as it is fed by the body and by this false physical personality. The soul is therefore prevented from living its true life and is compelled to get all its impressions in this way. Thus it is held down by the body, enchained, as it were.

The result of this condition is that one, that is a soul, is not able to hear about the things that he should hear, nor see the things that he should see. In other words, sight and hearing are permanently shut off from the true senses. Man sees not things as they are but as they seem to this distorted personality, and he hears not true sounds, or true words, but rather those distortions which the auditory apparatus communicate to consciousness. As

the body does not permit one to either see or hear
the true, it follows that he is shut off from reality
and is forced to live in that realm of psychic dis-
tortion. The soul ceases to act directly and in
fact lives only through the psychic reactions resulting from this impression of the senses. Thus it is
merely a psychical reaction growing out of the
distorted senses of the body. This life of psychical
reaction is in reality the cause of practically all the
ills with which we have to bear, and the direct
action of the soul becomes practically impossible,
as a result of this distorted life. From this we can
easily reach the conclusion that the first step in the
Hermetic Art must be the freeing of the soul from
dependence upon the body's senses. So long as the
soul depends upon the senses of the body it can
never escape this condition, which is the ground
of bad. Our Art, therefore, involves as its first
step the attainment of that state of unfoldment in
which the direct action of the soul is possible.
This is accomplished through the awakening of the
soul sense. That sense which enables the soul to
unite itself with Kosmic sense and thus to sense
the operations of Kosmic sense and hence see
things as they are and not as they seem. When the
soul's sense has been developed it must be united
with intuition, which is that faculty of the soul
enabling it to become in a way cognizant of Kosmic thoughts. Next the faculty of pure reason
must be developed, which will enable the soul to
analyze and synthesize the process of the Kosmic
mind. In this way the soul becomes enabled to
function independent of the body. To function
in direct connection with the soul plane of the
Kosmos. Therefore we have developed the direct
action of the soul, thus freeing it from those psychical reactions growing out of the operation of
physical sensation. When this has been accomplished the soul no longer depends upon the senses

for its knowledge and its concept of the world. It is now emancipated from the sway of sense engendered consciousness, having the direct soul consciousness. Thus in a sense it is free, emancipated, dwelling on its own plane and there being fully conscious.

After this has been attained we have then what is really the Great Work of the Hermetic Art, namely, the bringing of the body into harmony with the soul so that the soul acts directly upon the body, acting from within outward unto the end that the body's sense, instead of reacting under the vibrations from without, responds to the vibrations from within, with the result that the soul sense reproduces itself through the medium of the body sense. Thus the body's sense, instead of acting in the usual manner, in reality dramatizes the soul sense. Of course in order that this state may be realized we have to first develop the body through a process of transmutation or alchemicalization to the point where it will respond through its material atoms and molecules to the vibration of the soul. Of course this is never fully realized. However, as this process of transmutation goes on from day to day, it becomes more refined, more etherealized, more spiritualized, more subtle, until at last it reaches the point where it responds fairly well to the vibration of the soul. Thus the alchemy of the body is the next step in the Sacred Art which must be begun subsequent to the freeing of the soul from dependence upon the body. It will therefore be seen that the process is exactly reversed from what it is in the ordinary mind. The natural man is the one in whom the bodily senses control the soul, feed and instruct the soul from without, while the Artistic man is the one in whom the soul controls and dominates the body and its senses, causing them to reproduce in terms of physical sensation the consciousness of the soul.

All processes of bodily generation are therefore reversed. In the Artistic man they are controlled in all their operations by the generative activity of the soul, hence they are regenerated from within. Therefore the Artistic life is very often termed the regenerate life while the natural life is the generate life. This is the true key to the Hermetic Art as applied to the life of man.

Many people talk about getting back to nature, —about the natural life, the natural man, etc., but in our Art there is no such ideal. As a matter of fact we are striving through Art to save man from nature, to elevate him above the plane of what nature will produce, and thus through the regeneration of the whole being by the generative action of the soul to bring man into the higher estate; to make the ideal life practical by having all the emotions of his physical existence directly controlled by the force of ideas and ideals. This is the real process of Art. The Hermetic Artist is the one who is doing it, who is actually transmuting the body in accordance with the direct action of the soul. In a certain sense we have here a substitute for civilization and culture. Civilization and culture are an effort to change the nature of man, to redeem him from nature, to develop an artificial character in place of the natural character; but this is accomplished by civilization and culture independent of a knowledge of the soul life, independent of any concept of the interior life. Therefore the Hermetic Art produces something altogether different than does the force of civilization and culture, seeing that their efforts are from without to transform man into something other than his particular nature, while by Art we have the soul redeeming the man from nature; producing an artificial culture that is purely in accordance with the spirit. This is the real function of the Hermetic Art, which has as

its basic principle the transmutation of the body
unto the end that it may act as the vehicle for the
expression of the soul instead of the soul being the
internalization of the body.

The Hermetic Art

That No One of Existing Things Doth Perish,
But Men in Error Speak of Their Changes
as Destructions and as Deaths

TEXT

Parthey (G.), *Hermetis Trismegisti Poemander* (Berlin, 1854), 56-59.

Patrizzi (F.), *Nova de Universis Philosophia* (Venice, 1593), 48a, 48b.

Mead (G. R. S.), *Thrice Greatest Hermes* (London, 1906), Corpus Hermeticum VIII (IX).

1. [*Hermes*]. Concerning Soul and Body, son, we now must speak; in what way Soul is deathless, and whence comes the activity in composing and dissolving Body.

For there's no *death* for aught of things [that are]; the thought [this] word conveys, is either void of fact, or [simply] by the knocking off a syllable what is called "death," doth stand for "deathless."

For death is of destruction, and nothing in the Cosmos is destroyed. For if Cosmos is second God, a life that cannot die, it cannot be that any part of this immortal life should die. All things in Cosmos are parts of Cosmos, and most of all is man, the rational animal.

2. For truly first of all, eternal and transcending birth, is God the universals' Maker. Second is he after His image, Cosmos, brought into being by Him, sustained and fed by Him, made deathless, as by his own Sire, living for aye, as ever free from death.

Now that which ever-liveth, differs from the Eternal; for He hath not been brought to being *by another*, and even if He hath been *brought to being*, He hath not *been* brought into being by Himself, but ever *is* brought into being.

For the Eternal, in that It is Eternal, is the all. The Father is Himself eternal *of* Himself, but Cosmos hath become eternal and immortal *by* the Father.

3. And of the matter stored beneath it, the Father made of it a universal body, and packing it together made it spherical—wrapping it round the life—[a sphere] which is immortal in itself, that doth make materiality eternal.

But He, the Father, full-filled with His ideas, did sow the lives into the sphere, and shut them in as in a cave, willing to order forth the life with every kind of living.

So He with deathlessness enclosed the universal body, that matter might not wish to separate itself from body's composition, and so dissolve into its own [original] unorder.

For matter, son, when it was yet incorpo-rate, was in unorder. And it doth still retain down here this [nature of unorder] envolving the rest of the small lives—that increase-and-decrease which men call death.

4. It is round earthly lives that this unorder doth exist. For that the bodies of the heavenly ones preserve one order allotted to them from the Father as their rule; and it is by the restoration of each one [of them] this order is preserved indissolute.

The "restoration" then of bodies on the earth is [thus their] composition, whereas their dissolution restores them to those bodies which can never be dissolved, that is to say, which know no death. Privation, thus, of sense is brought about, not loss of bodies.

5. Now the third life—Man, after the image of the Cosmos made, [and] having mind, after the Father's will, beyond all earthly lives—not only doth have feeling with the second God, but also hath concep-tion of the first; for of the one 'tis sensible as of a body, while of the other it conceives as bodieless and the Good Mind.

Tat. Doth then *this* life not perish?

Her. Hush, son! and understand what God, what Cosmos [is], what is a life that cannot die, and what a life subject to disso-lution.

Yea, understand the Cosmos is by God and in God; but Man by Cosmos and in Cosmos.

The source and limit and the constitution of all things is God.

LESSON III

Soul and Body

1. (*Hermes*): Concerning Soul and
Body, son, we now must speak; in what way
Soul is deathless, and whence comes the
activity in composing and dissolving Body.

For there's no death for aught of things
[that are]; the thought [this] word conveys,
is either void of Body, or [simply] by the
knocking off of a syllable what is called
[death], doth stand for [deathless].

For death is of destruction, and nothing
in the Cosmos is destroyed. For if Cosmos
is second God, a life that cannot die, it cannot be that any part of this immortal life
should die. All things in Cosmos are parts
of Cosmos and most of all is man, the
rational animal.

(*Hermes*): Concerning Soul and Body,
son, we now must speak; in what way Soul
is deathless, and whence comes the activity
in composing and dissolving Body.

The subject of this sermon is the relation of the
soul and the body. Both principles are introduced
into the discussion. The discussion relates itself
to the way in which the soul is deathless, or immortal, and the sources of the activity composing and
dissolving the body. We therefore find that the
subject involved here is the immortal or deathless
nature of the soul taken in conjunction with the
mortality and transformations of the body. He

43

indicates that there is an activity operating in the body which both composes and dissolves the body. Hence it follows that it is the same activity that composes or constructs the body that also dissolves it. We must therefore see in physical dissolution or so-called death, the disintegration of the physical structure into the material elements of which it is composed. Death is, therefore, the dissolving of the body into the different elements that go to construct it. In other words the body is organized from previously existing elements, and death is the dissolution of this organism into the elements which previously constructed it. Hence it means nothing more than that those elements which in the body's life were organic become inorganic through death. At the same time we are instructed that this transformation does not touch the soul life, the soul being in no sense influenced by such disintegrating process.

For there's no death for aught of things [that are]; the thought [this] word conveys, is either void of body, or [simply] by the knocking off of a syllable what is called [death], doth stand for [deathless].

The contention made here is that there is no death for any real thing, for any of the things that are. This does not only relate to the human soul but to everything else, to every organism. There is no such thing as death. What has once been produced must forever remain. Immortality in this sense is therefore extended to all things. He goes so far as to contend that death is synonymous with the deathless, that it can have no other meaning than deathless. He contends that as a matter of fact nothing dies. He is not speaking here of any transcendental ideas, he does not represent idealism when he says there is no death; he denies the

fact of death; stating plainly and emphatically that
nothing dies, as a matter of fact; therefore we
must not look upon this statement as being an
expression of any transcendental idealism, as being
spiritually understood, but he is stating as a matter of physical science that nothing dies.

For death is of destruction, and nothing
in the Cosmos is destroyed. For if Cosmos
is second God, a life that cannot die, it cannot be that any part of this immortal life
should die. All things in Cosmos are parts
of Cosmos and most of all is man, the
rational animal.

In this paragraph he undertakes to explain why
it is that there can be no death. His reason is that
death partakes of destruction. All death, in the
true sense of the term, would be a destruction, and
he states that nothing in the Kosmos is ever
destroyed. From this we come to his argument,
and his position is that Kosmos is second God. He
therefore calls our attention to his doctrine of the
three Gods. That is to say, the Absolute God, and
the Kosmos as His manifestation and hence the
second God,—the image of God in another sense,—
and man as the third God. Now the Kosmos is
the second God in the sense that it is the direct
manifestation of the unmanifest God. In a certain sense it is the manifest God. Being the manifestation of God he holds that in order for the
Kosmos to die it would be necessary for the manifestation of God to cease, because the Kosmos in
the Hermetic view of the case, is not a permanent
thing in the sense of something once produced that
forever remains, but rather is a something perpetually changing; a state of perpetual manifestation;
the process of the ever-becoming manifest of the

activities and attributes of the unmanifest God. This being the case, Kosmos is nothing other than the mirroring in Hyle of the activities of Ku, the Motherhood of God; its divine essence in all its activities becoming mirrored in substance that constitutes Kosmos in the true sense of the word. Now Kosmos must continue as long as the activities of the unmanifest God continue to be mirrored in substance. Those activities must continue to be so mirrored as long as they subsist. In other words, in order that Kosmos might cease it would be necessary that the Absolute God should cease to make or to express itself actively, and as the unmanifest God exists or rather subsists only in the act of coming into manifestation it follows that were it to cease such activity it would die. Therefore the Absolute God would have to become extinct before Kosmos could ever become extinct. Kosmos is therefore as eternal as is the life of God. For this reason he says that Kosmos is a life that cannot die. It is a life that cannot die because it is the continuation on a lower plane of the life of God himself, therefore Kosmos cannot possibly cease to be. It ever must be. This being the case Kosmos is an immortal life, being but a reflection of the life of God, the immortality of the Divinity is therefore continued in the immortality of the Kosmos. It cannot therefore be that this immortal life should die seeing that it is immortal, as it is completely bound up and inseparably merged in the immortality of the Divine Life, because Kosmos is not distinct from God. Kosmos is but the externalization and manifestation of the life of the unmanifest God.

He further states that all things in Kosmos are parts of Kosmos; and in this we have a distinctly Hermetic doctrine. A great many schools of philosophy have held that Kosmos was some sort of a metaphysical thing, a substratum to things, and that things were distinct from Kosmos. But

this is not the Hermetic view. Hermes teaches
that Kosmos is nothing other than the sum total of
all things born. It must here be borne in mind
that he repudiates the idea of creation and replaces
it with the idea of birth. In other words, all things
are born out of Ku and as such are born of God,—
not created,—and being brought forth they are in
Kosmos and Kosmos is the sum total of all such
births. Kosmos is twofold; it is the act of being
born, the continuous sequence of being born, and
at the same time it includes the things born.
Hermes was far too scientific to make any distinction between the act of being born and the things
that are born, because it is evident that if there
was not an act of being born there would be nothing born and that no act of bearing can fail to
result in a birth. Hence Kosmos is both the production of things and the sum total of the things
produced. Were we to eliminate all the things in
Kosmos there would be nothing left of Kosmos.
Kosmos would cease to be. Inasmuch, therefore,
as Kosmos is the mirroring of the activity of God
in Hyle it follows that such mirroring can only
take place in the production of things as the formal
expression of the divine action. Hence the divine
life lives in the act of producing all things, and
likewise in all the things thus produced. Therefore all things in Kosmos are parts of Kosmos and
Kosmos is nothing other than the sum total of all
things engendered. Now, inasmuch as Kosmos is
immortal life and that life consists in the perpetual
continuity of the process of engendering things, it
follows that the thing engendered by a deathless
process must in the nature of things be deathless.
Undoubtedly it may change its form from time to
time but it will never cease to be because its ultimate origin is the divine thought. The divine
being deathless, eternal, immortal, all of its
thoughts must be deathless, eternal and immortal.

As a deathless, eternal, immortal thought has set in motion the activity that engenders a thing, it must be that that activity will be continuous, as continuous as is the thought that set in motion such activity. This being true it will follow that the activity that engendered the thing being continuous, the life of the thing resulting from such engendering activity must likewise be continuous; hence the immortality of all things engendered is clearly demonstrated.

And most of all is man, the rational animal. More than anything else is man the recipient of this eternal life, for the reason that man is the most complicated and the highest manifestation of this creative process. Of all things engendered man comes nearer to the divine prototype than anything else, and the reason for this is clearly shown, that he is a rational animal, he is the one animal endowed with reason. Now reason here must not be confused with what is ordinarily termed reason,—that is the capacity to learn by experience, to reach conclusions from data. That is not the reason of which Hermes speaks. To him reason is the pure, *a priori* reason, that has nothing to do with data but reasons from Universals to particulars. This is his concept of reason. Man is the rational animal. That is to say, he is the one and only animal endowed with this capacity to reason from cause to effect. As this reason is that which produces all things, is the creative wisdom that has produced everything, it follows that in his reason man is divine, he partakes of the nature of God, he is endowed with the creative power and for that reason, partaking more than any other of the attributes of divinity, he therefore approaches nearer to the divine life of God than anything else. Hence he possesses a greater measure of divinity and hence of immortality than does anything else. Therefore above all kosmic things is man deathless, immortal, eternal.

In this we have the suggestion of the Hermetic Art. Man's reason is the creative power resident within him. By the cultivation of that creative power he is able to become a creator himself to the extent that his Creative power has been awakened. Therefore it is through the cultivation of the reason that man is able to reach this exalted state. The Hermetic Art is therefore attained through the cultivation of the human reason. Such rational awakening is therefore the way to the attainment of the art of creation.

2. For truly first of all, eternal and transcending birth, is God the Universals' Maker. Second is he [after His image], Cosmos, brought into being by Him, sustained and fed by Him, made deathless, as by his own Sire, living for aye, as ever free from death.

Now that which ever liveth, differs from the Eternal, for He hath not been brought to being *by another,* and even if He have been *brought to being,* He hath not *been* brought into being by Himself, but ever *is* brought into being.

For the Eternal, in that It is eternal, is the all. The Father is Himself eternal of Himself, but Cosmos hath become eternal and immortal *by* the Father.

For truly first of all, eternal and transcending birth, is God the universal's Maker. Second is he [after his image], Cosmos, brought into being by Him, sustained and

fed by Him, made deathless, as by his own
Sire, living for aye, as ever free from death.

The first and ultimate principle is God, the universal's Maker. By the universals he means those
verities which are everywhere the same and which
are interchangeable. The term is used in contra-
distinction to particulars. In this we have a fundamental principle of the ancient philosophy. The
two principles below God are universals and particulars. By particulars is meant things and the
processes engendering particular things. By the
universals they mean those processes which are not
in any sense particular, which relate to all things
without distinction. These universals are to a
certain extent identical with the Great Supernal
Gods, though not exactly. Now God is spoken of
as the maker of the universals. That is to say the
universals came into being through their having
been emanated from God. In other words, the
universals are the fundamental attributes of God
projected into manifestations through Kosmos.
Now this God, the universals' maker, is the first
of all, because all particulars come from universals
and all universals come from God. Therefore He
is first of all because all things proceed either directly or indirectly from Him. Eternal and transcending birth, because all births emanate from
Him. As He is the bearer of all that is there is
nothing left to bear Him. He cannot be born
because all things are born by Him, therefore
He transcends birth. In this sense it would be
somewhat more correct to say She, because the
God alluded to here is Ku, the feminine divine
essence. After this God, we come to the second.
Second is He after His image. After His image,—
that is the Kosmos. Kosmos is after the image of
God, because, in the true sense of the word, it is
God's image, that is, it is God made manifest, and

this comes forth out of God. It is brought into being by God, is sustained and fed by Him. That is to say, it has no source of existence, apart from God, is absolutely dependent upon God for all things, and is not only brought into being, but is continuously sustained and fed and nourished by God. In other words, Kosmos has not been brought into being by God, but is in continuous process of being brought into being by Him. As God is indeed and in truth the Father and Mother of Kosmos, it must be that Kosmos will partake of the nature of his Father and Mother, consequently Kosmos has been made deathless by his Sire. That is made deathless in and through the very process of having been brought into being by the Father. Living for aye, as ever free from death, because the kosmic life is continuous and uninterruptedly sustained by the life of God.

Now that which ever-liveth, differs from the Eternal; for He hath not been brought to being *by another,* and even if He have been *brought to being,* He hath not *been* brought into being by Himself, but ever *is* brought into being.

He draws some very fine distinctions here. For instance, he draws the distinction between the everliving and the Eternal. The ever-living is not the same as the Eternal, and he shows the distinction. The Eternal hath not been brought into being by another, and even if the Eternal has been brought into being, He hath not been brought into being by Himself. That is to say, the Eternal cannot create Himself, and this self-creation would not constitute eternity, but this of which he speaks ever is brought into being. There is the process of perpetual bringing into being and there is this fine distinction which must always be borne in mind, eternity is beginningless and endless, though the ever-living may have a beginning, but it can never have an end. But the Eternal is in perpetuity to infinity, both backward and forward; ever is being brought into being, and yet this is not something that has always been stable, it is something in perpetual process of coming into being and yet the process is from infinity to infinity.

For the Eternal, in that It is eternal, is the all. The Father is Himself eternal *of* Himself, but Cosmos hath become eternal and immortal *by* the Father.

This is the difference, both the Father and Mother on the one hand and Kosmos on the other are eternal, Æonian. But there is a distinction, the Eternal, in that it is eternal, that is in Its character of eternity, is the all, there can be no particularity. Being eternal, though the particular may be ever-living, yet it can never be eternal. But the eternal must in the very nature of things be limitless. The Father-Mother, the Absolute God, is Himself eternal of Himself. That is to say, His eternity is engendered from Himself or of Himself. In other words, His nature or energy is eternal and therefore in no sense dependent upon anything else. In a word, God is not subject to generation, is in no sense generated by anything else. He is the ingenerate whose eternity subsists in His action. Being in His action eternal, He is dependent upon nothing apart from Himself. The Kosmos, however, has become eternal and immortal by the Father. In other words, it is the reflection of the immortality and eternity of the Father in substance that constitutes the eternity and immortality of the Kosmos. Kosmos is eternal and immortal because it is the active manifestation of an eternal and immortal verity. It is this which makes Kosmos eternal. Kosmos, in other words, is eternally generated, while the eternity of the Father is self-subsistent and not subject to generation. In a word, were all else to be blotted out God would still be eternal, but were God to be blotted out Kosmos would cease to be. The eternity of the Kosmos is therefore conferred eternity. One that lives in Kosmos is the result of another Eternity, but the Eternity of God is absolute. At the same time, the one is as eternal as the other. Kosmos cannot disappear during the eternity of God. It is also beginningless and endless. At the same time it is an eternity that is perpetually being induced, but this is Kosmos as a whole that possesses this Eternity. The different parts of Kosmos are everliving but not eternal.

LESSON IV

The Eternity of Matter

3. And of the matter stored beneath it, the Father made of it a universal body, and packing it together made it spherical—wrapping it round the life—[a sphere] which is immortal in itself, and that doth make materiality eternal.

But He, the Father, full-filled with His ideas, did sow the lives into the sphere, and shut them in as in a cave, willing to order forth the life with every kind of living.

So He with deathlessness enclosed the universal body, that matter might not wish to separate itself from body's composition, and so dissolve into its own [original] unorder.

For matter, son, when it was yet incorporate, was in unorder. And it doth still retain down here this [nature of unorder]' evolving the rest of the small lives—that increase-and-decrease which men call death.

And of the matter stored beneath it, the Father made of it a universal body, and packing it together made it spherical—wrapping it round the life—[a sphere] which is immortal in itself, and that doth make materiality eternal.

After speaking of the nature of Kosmos, Hermes next comes to the consideration of the matter stored beneath Kosmos. We must bear in mind that at

55

the time of which he speaks, matter was in a state of chaos, for there was neither form nor order manifested in this sub-kosmic matter. We are informed that of the matter stored beneath Kosmos, the Father made a universal body. That is to say, by the action of the divine power, working through the instrumentality of the Kosmic Powers, the chaotic matter beneath the Kosmos was gathered together into one body which was to constitute the universe. This voluminous body of matter was packed together and concentrated into a massive body. It was given a spherical form. It was in fact a universal Egg, which was to contain all things of the universe within its depths and from it they were each and all to be hatched forth into individual life. It was given this spherical form by wrapping the matter round the life which was within its depths. The universe is therefore in the form of a hollow sphere within the depths of which is enclosed the life which therefore gives forth life to all parts of the universal shell. Because the universal life is enfolded within the universal form this life is continually vitalizing the entire structure of the universe, and thus the universe becomes a body that is immortal in itself. It does not derive its immortality from without, but from the life enclosed by itself. Because of the life which is continually renewing and vitalizing the universal body, both in whole and in part, materiality is made eternal, and hence is organized matter in the universe immortal by reason of the life which it contains, this is the true cause of the eternity of matter.

But He, the Father, full-filled with His ideas, did sow the lives into the sphere, and shut them in as in a cave, willing to order forth the life with every kind of living.

The Father being filled to the full with His ideas; for the nature of the Father is to think, and hence He lives in His ideas; His thinking tends at all times to radiate His ideas, and in this way to diffuse them through all space. This being the case, the lives were sown within the universal sphere. They were received within the sphere, and were there enclosed so that they might not escape. These lives must not be confounded with the life that was enclosed within the sphere in the beginning. Neither must they be confused with the small lives. They are rather the great lives, or the material Gods. They are the Vital and the Etherial Gods as well as the Terrene Gods. They are therefore enclosed within the sphere, so that it will not be possible for them to separate themselves from the universal sphere. They were enclosed in the sphere that they might order forth, or send forth in accordance with order, the enclosed life, causing it to assume every form of living, that is, to differentiate itself into the diverse lives that will give life to all forms of living things. It is this life as the germ that causes all species to come into being in the earth. This is the true explanation of the monadic origin of all the diverse forms of terrene life, and this is the sense in which every thing has come from a germ in the earth. It is also to be borne in mind that while this is an account of the creation of the universe, at the same time all the spheres were formed in the same manner, and all this applies to the earth as well as to the entire universe. Thus it is true that it is the ordering forth of the enclosed life, under the impulse of the lives that causes all the forms of living things to come into being on the earth. They are literally born from within the depths of the earth. The earth is in fact the Mother and the fecund womb from which all forms of living things are born, after they have been conceived and gestated within her maternal womb. Thus is the earth literally the mother of all things earthly, and not merely in a figurative sense.

So He with deathlessness enclosed the universal body, that matter might not wish to separate itself from body's composition, and so dissolve into its own [original] unorder.

Because the life was enclosed within the universal body, and because the great lives or the lesser Gods were sown within the earth, and the life became active, it followed that the universal body was enclosed with deathlessness, seeing that it was the vehicle for the manifestation of deathless powers, it followed that the body itself was made deathless. Matter is therefore eternally united with the composition of universal body, and can no more separate itself from it, hence, matter can only exist in the composition of the universal body. All matter must exist in the composition of bodies, and can never exist in any other way. Thus, organized matter can never be dissolved into the state of unorder from which it has come into order, but can only remain under the form of organized bodies.

For matter, son, when it was yet incorporate, was in unorder. And it doth still retain down here this [nature of unorder] enveloping the rest of the small lives—that increase-and-decrease which men call death.

Before matter was incorporated, it was in a state of unorder. It was the incorporation of matter, so that it became corporate, that is, a part of the universal body, that brought it into the state of

order. While down here, that is, on the physical
plane, this nature of unorder, still persists in matter, for physical matter is not subject to the control
of the Kosmic Powers as is the matter of finer
grades. Because of this condition, the rest of the
small lives, that is the life principle of every living
thing springing from the life contained within the
earth, are enveloped in this matter in its state of
unorder, and for this reason are they all subject to
the process of increase-and-decrease which men
call death. Because the matter of the earth does
not freely respond to the transformative processes
of the higher powers, the changes in it may not be
spontaneous as they are above. This being true,
corporeal bodies in the earth experience are bound
to pass through periods of increase, after which
they must experience a process of decrease. This
is due to the fact that the two processes are not
permitted to go on simultaneously, and in equal
proportions, but there must be a period of increase,
followed by a period of decrease. It is this which
leads to the throwing off of the outer shell, when it
has survived its usefulness, and this men in their
ignorance call death. This teaches us a very important lesson in the Hermetic Art. Death as it
is vulgarly called, is due to the fact that a body
is built up of such gross matter, and held together
in such rigidity that the forces cannot manifest
freely through it, and hence the transformations
are not permitted to go on within it as rapidly as
is its construction, hence, after a time, these life
forces, being unable to so transform it, as to manifest through it as a vehicle, will become destructive,
and hence the dissolution of that form will result.
Death, simply means that life forces are not made
use of in their normal action, and hence being
permitted to accumulate through uselessness and
idleness, they become, in time, disintegrative. The
cure for death is therefore to preserve a perfect

balance between the forces of growth and of disintegration. So long as this is kept up, one will not only not die, but he will grow no older. All the energy within the body must at all times be made use of. None of it must ever be permitted to remain idle for a single moment. If it is utilized at all times, it will in this way act constructively at all times, and hence there will be no decrease, as well as no increase, but at all times the perfect equilibrium will be maintained, hence there will be no death.

4. It is round earthly lives that this unorder doth exist. For that the bodies of the heavenly ones preserve one order allotted to them from the Father as their rule; and it is by the restoration of each one [of them] this order is preserved indissolute.

The "restoration" then of bodies on the earth is [thus their] composition, whereas their dissolution restores them to those bodies which can never be dissolved, that is to say, which know no death. Privation, thus, of sense is brought about, not loss of bodies.

It is round earthly lives that this unorder doth exist. For that the bodies of the heavenly ones preserve one order allotted to them from the Father as their rule; and it is by the restoration of each one [of them] this order is preserved indissolute.

This state of unorder is confined to earthly lives, for they only are encumbered with envelopes of matter so gross that this order cannot manifest

through them in all of their actions. The heavenly
ones, are those lives above the earth plane. They
preserve the order allotted to them from the
Father, in that they are all the time responsive to
the urge of that power which has descended from
the Father and which operates through them,
causing them to act in accordance with that order.
Owing to the Cyclic Law, all such heavenly bodies
are from time to time restored to their original
status, and hence this order which governs them
is perpetually preserved and can never be dissolved. This will be true of any body that at all
times responds to the Cyclic Law. This Law causes
all these bodies to return to their original condition
and thus to become renewed, and hence there is
no reason why the form of the body should ever
become changed. This is due to the fact that all
such renewals take place within the body and
hence no cause is there for the discarding of body
in order that a change may take place by the ex-
changing of one body for another. This is true
of the heavenly bodies because of their subtle
nature, and of their receptivity to all the movements of the heavenly order operating through
them. It would be the same in the case of earthly
bodies were they equally responsive to the movements of the heavenly order.

The "Restoration" then of bodies on the
earth is [thus their] composition, whereas
their dissolution restores them to those
bodies which can never be dissolved, that is
to say, which know no death. Privation,
thus, of sense is brought about, not loss of
bodies.

He here most distinctly teaches the doctrine of
the "restoration" or reincarnation, of all earthly

bodies. The composition of a body is the restoration to earthly embodiment, of a body which previously existed on the earth in the form of a corporeal earthly body. This leads us to the conclusion that the corporeal earthly body is not the only body which earthly things possess. The dissolution of the earthly body is the process which restores the earthly embodied thing to a body which can never be dissolved. This means that when the earthly body is dissolved, the life which was embodied in it enters and manifests through a body that is subject to the heavenly order, the same as are the heavenly bodies, hence, to a heavenly body. Of course this indicates that all earth life is in possession of heavenly bodies as well as of earthly bodies. The latter is lost from time to time through dissolution, to be again restored through "restoration" or reincarnation, but the heavenly body can never be dissolved. Death is then confined to the periodical deprivation of the earthly body, but does not affect the heavenly body. The earthly body is of importance in that it is the vehicle through which an earthly life is sensible of things on the earth. When the life is deprived of this earthly body, it is deprived of all sense of the earthly realm for the reason that the heavenly body is not sensible of earthly things. As it has no vehicle of consciousness for the earthly environment, it knows nothing through the medium of sense, of the earth, hence the earthly sense is lost, but it is not deprived of a body, seeing that the heavenly body continues. Thus we see that nothing in this universe can exist apart from a body, and the body will be the kind fitted to serve in the mode of life which any thing is manifesting at the time. But nothing exists at all at any time, without existing in a body of some order.

LESSON V

The Life of Man

Now the third life—Man, after the image of the Cosmos made, [and] having mind, after the Father's will, beyond all earthly lives—not only doth have feeling with the second God, but also hath conception of the first; for of the one 'tis sensible as of a body, while of the other it conceives as bodiless and the Good Mind.

Tat. Doth then this life not perish?

Her. Hush, son! and understand what God, what Cosmos [is], what is a life that cannot die, and what a life subject to dissolution.

Yea, understand the Cosmos is by God and in God; but Man by Cosmos and in Cosmos.

The source and limit and constitution of all things is God.

Now the third life—Man, after the image of the Cosmos made, [and] having mind, after the Father's will, beyond all earthly lives—not only doth have feeling with the second God, but also hath conception of the first; for of the one 'tis sensible as of a body, while of the other it conceives as bodiless and the Good Mind.

The three lives spoken of here are the life of God, including the Kosmos viewed from a certain

63

aspect, but more properly it relates to God alone; the second life is the Kosmos and the things proceeding from it; the third life is Man. That is, used in the sense of generic man, man as a species, but also relating to the individual man. We are informed that he is after the image of the Kosmos made—that is to say the third life, man, is made after the image of the Kosmos. We must always guard against the error of assuming that man is made after the image of God. This is not true. The Man made after the image of God is the Kosmos, and to a certain extent the Anthropos, but the man that we know of through experience, the human being, is made after the image of the Kosmos and not after the image of God. One special characteristic of man is that he has mind after the Father's will, beyond all earthly lives. That is to say the human mind has been produced by the Father's will. That is the Mind of the Father expressing itself dynamically as will, that is as the will of the Father is mind becoming active and dynamic will force which enters the Kosmos and acts upon man through its kosmic manifestation evolves mind in man. Man's mind, therefore, is not of the earth earthly, not evolved from matter, but is rather descended from the Father through the Kosmos into man. While to a certain extent mind, using intellect here as a department of mind, is common to all earthly lives, yet man possesses mind beyond all earthly lives; not only does he possess a superior quantity of mind, but also a superior and higher quality, a more spiritual quality of mind, than what any of the animals possess. This superior quality of mind is easily distinguished from the quality of mind present in the animal creation.

The animal mind is characterized by the ability to learn by experience; all that the animal knows he has acquired through experience and observation. His reason is *a posteriori* in every sense of the word. Man's mind transcends that of the animal in that he is not dependent upon the testimony of his physical senses and upon his physical experiences for knowledge. Man's mind becomes almost divine in that he is able to dispense with sensation entirely, to dispense with the concrete and enter the realm of pure abstraction. The power of abstract thinking is truly what characterizes the human mentality as human. The ability to think in abstractions is a clear demonstration of the divinity of the mind of man. That is the divinity of the minds of such men as are able to think in abstractions. Those who cannot rise to abstraction of course still have the mentalities of the animals. And as it is this human mind that differentiates man from the animal creation, it will logically follow that all men who are capable of thinking in the concrete only are animals, brute beasts and not yet human. It is for this reason that the ancient philosophers became so enthusiastic over mind, over the power of thought, because they clearly realized that this power of abstract thinking was something that was not possessed by the animal, hence it was something definitely characteristic of man as man. For this reason they very strongly emphasized the importance of the intellect.

Not only doth this man have feeling with the second God, that is the Kosmos, but he also has conception of the first. Notice this distinction therefore. Man has feeling with the second God, —that is to say the developed man has the same sense that the Kosmos has, that is to say it is well within the range of man's evolution to evolve kosmic sense, not only the physical sense but the kosmic sense, which will therefore give him the same feeling that the Kosmos has. Also he is able to have a mental conception of the first God, the

Absolute. Man is able to conceive of God, the One and only One, through his mind, but he cannot be sensible of this first God, he has no sense by which he can approach the first God, but approaches Him only through the conception of the mind. However, he can through sense feel the second God, or the Kosmos. The second God, or the Kosmos, is sensible as of a body, while the other is conceivable as bodiless, as the Good Mind. Therefore man is not required to merely think and theorize of the Kosmos but through the evolution of kosmic sense he is able to sense the Kosmos, to make it sensible to him as though it was a body, to feel its presence. By reason of this kosmic sense it becomes, as it were, objective, so that the development of this kosmic sense enables one to become sensible, conscious of the Kosmos. This, however, is not the case when we come to God. God is conceived only as bodiless and the Good Mind. God, therefore, can be conceived of only in our thought; we can think of God but we cannot sense Him. We think of God first as being bodiless, as having no form, no corporeality, as being a condition of infinite and universal diffusion. Until one has conceived of God in this sense, as energy, universally present and more than universally present, he has not conceived of God at all. Second, we must conceive of God as the Good Mind, as Mind and Ku, as that mind which engenders all things by its thought, as Absolute Mind. And only can we think of God under these two aspects, universally diffused energy, formless, and as the Good Mind, the Absolute Intelligence. And this is purely a mental concept; therefore God can subsist to no one other than as a concept of the mind.

Let this point be clearly borne in mind and we will see the fallacy of most of the religions, for most religions are predicated upon the theory that man can approach God through sense; that he can sense or feel God; that it is possible for us to feel through the cultivation of our love nature, through the development of our affectional nature, through a yearning, a longing, a reaching out of the heart, that one can find God. Such a view is utterly fallacious, for God is not subject to sense; he cannot be found through sensation; the heart can never find God. Man alone is capable of grasping God, and it grasps Him through thought and in no other way. It follows, therefore, that those people who profess to have found God in some other way, know absolutely nothing of the God beyond-all-name. What they are really worshiping is the second God, the Kosmos, which they have found through sense. Their religion being sensible and not intelligible, it follows that they are worshiping the second God, the Kosmos, and that there is no trace of a devotion to the first God, the Good Mind, in all the conceptions which they hold. This will show the reason why there are so many difficulties in the way of inculcating the religion of the mind. The religion of the senses has taken such possession of the people that they have no thought for the religion of the mind. The real trouble is very few people know how to think independent of sense. The all important thing, therefore, is for man to develop this capacity for supersensuous thinking. And that is the reason why the Gnostic has always insisted upon the development of this mind power; the subjection of all religious questions to philosophical analysis.

Tat. Doth then *this* life not perish?

We have here the question introduced as to whether the life of man perishes or does not. This of course is a very important question as the immortality of everything is the burden of the sermon, as the teaching is that no one of existing things does perish. The question then is as to whether the life of man is an exception to this rule or whether this rule applies in the life of man the same as in everything else.

Her. Hush, son, and understand what God, what Cosmos [is], what is a life that cannot die, and what a life subject to dissolution.

Hermes orders Tat to hush, for it is very evident that he has not grasped the meaning of the teaching given in the entire sermon otherwise he would not ask such a fool question. His remark shows that Tat has not thought deeply on what he had to say; that he has not paid the proper attention, has not discriminated properly; for he admonishes him to understand what God is, what the Kosmos is and what a life is that cannot die and also the nature of a life subject to dissolution. Had he carefully discriminated on these points and gotten a proper understanding of these four heads of the subject, he would have been in no quandary whatsoever as to the meaning of his father. The first head of the discourse is of the nature of God, the second head is of the nature of the Kosmos, the third head is the nature of a deathless life and the fourth head is the nature of life subject to dissolution. All these have been thoroughly explained in the preceding portions of the sermon, hence it is evident that Tat has not paid proper heed to the instructions of his father under those four heads, else he would have had no difficulty in knowing where to place man.

Yea, understand the Cosmos is by God and in God; but Man is by Cosmos and in Cosmos.

We are assured that Kosmos is by God and in God; that is to say the Kosmos is perpetually in process of coming into being by reason of the life of God. God's thought and will, all the motions of his life, manifest as Kosmos, therefore the source of Kosmos is the active life of God. The word Kosmos means a picture, and it means this because the thought and action of God takes form as Kosmos, so that Kosmos is in reality a photograph of God, a living photograph, but nevertheless a photograph of God. Thus it ever comes into being by reason of the active life of God, and it subsists in God because it is but the expression in form of the divine thought and active life of God. Therefore it must be completely permeated and surrounded, enveloped as it were, by God's spirit, and takes form there. Now if it is true that the Kosmos is but the mirroring in form of the thought and life of God, it must partake of the nature of that divine thought and life and above all inasmuch as the thought and life of God can only manifest in terms of Kosmos and must manifest in that form, it will follow that as long as God thinks and makes he must make Kosmos. Furthermore we are assured by Hermes in other sermons that God subsists solely and entirely in thinking things and in making them, that is the very energy of God, hence were God to cease to think and to make he would cease to be. Now Kosmos is what he makes, therefore were he to cease to make Kosmos he would cease to be. Hence Kosmos is as eternal as God. Therefore the nature of Kosmos must be deathless and imperishable.

Man is by Kosmos and in Kosmos. That is to say, man exists within the Kosmos and as a result of the activity of the Kosmos. Now it follows that the Kosmos being the expression of God must duplicate on a lower plane the act of God. Hence it will follow that as God makes Kosmos as his nature is to make and as the nature of Kosmos is to duplicate the work of God, therefore it is in the nature of Kosmos to make. Man existing by Kosmos means that man exists because of the kosmic action, Kosmos being the reflection of the generative power of God it must follow that Kosmos likewise generates; if Kosmos generates man exists by reason of the generative action of Kosmos, hence man is the microcosm of the macrosmic Kosmos. Therefore the nature of man must be the exact duplicate of the nature of the Kosmos, hence man will have the same nature as has the Kosmos. As the Kosmos is eternal as God, because it is the reflection of God, so is man as eternal as the Kosmos because he is the work, the effect, the mirroring in individual form of the Kosmos itself. Hence life is imperishable, indestructible, immortal, eternal. He therefore demonstrates the eternity of the life of man and hence that it cannot perish. And this is true simply because man is the expression of Kosmic life.

The source and limit and the constitution of all things is in God.

The source of things abides in God, because things come into existence, because they exist out of God. They come into existence through God's thinking things manifest, or thinking them into manifestation. The particular thought of God acting upon Ku, or the divine essence, must engender that which corresponds to the thought, and that entering into Kosmos exists through and engenders that which corresponds to it, and so all things in general and each thing in particular is the direct result of the particular thought of God which has engendered it, therefore is God the source of all things. The limit of things is found also in God because nothing can come into existence which does not subsist in God. There is no other source of generic life. In no other way can life come into being. Therefore the thinking of God is the limit of all things; nothing can ever come into being unless God has thought of it; hence there exists nothing which is not contained in the thought of God, which God, therefore, has not prepared. He being the one and only source he is therefore the limit of everything for nothing can come into being without having been engendered by God. Thus we see that dualism, the doctrine of a power independent of and separate from the will of God is absolutely fallacious. All religions based upon a dualistic concept must therefore fall down because they assume a power apart from God. But as there is no generative power but what itself has been generated by God and but what has a generative power subject to the control of the generative power of God, it follows that there is nothing but what God has directly or indirectly engendered. Therefore the limit of all things is in God. The constitution of all things is in God, because all things are constituted in and through the divine thought and action of God. Having constituted each and everything it follows naturally that the constitution of each and everything is in God and they have no constitution independent of God. Therefore we are forced to the conclusion that God is really all in all. There exists and subsists nothing but God. His thought, his generative action, and that which they have engendered. So in the last analysis God is all there is. We have but God and his infinite mutations.

This truth is of the utmost importance in our study of the Hermetic Art, because it teaches us that the originating principle in all things is God, and further that this originating principle which we see as God, is thought; that the beginning of everything is thought; and second, the energy through which that can perfectly manifest itself.

Thought operating through energy and substance adapted to itself engenders by reason of such interactivity of thought, energy and substance, a dynamic power, an active force, which being the expression of that must absolutely correspond to that thought, and this in turn makes manifest the thing thought of, or rather the thought itself in terms of form. This, then, is the creative principle, this is the art of creation, and when we have learned to make our thought operate through the medium of energy and substance and operating that way to engender dynamic action manifesting in form, we have discovered the Art of Creation. Creative thought is the real creative power, but to be creative it must work in conjunction with energy and substance. Man by the application of this law can create himself anew, has within him the power of his own regeneration, and regeneration is to be accomplished in no other way. Man's salvation is, therefore, in making his thought sufficiently dynamic to perpetually recreate his body. The regeneration of this is accomplished by making thought energetic and substantial and causing it to act upon them. Thought must be the generative force, but it must act through energy and substance otherwise it is barren. The same principle which is here enunciated is also applicable to the physical aspect of the Great Work. If you will ponder carefully on what we say you will understand how a chemical application of these principles may be brought about, and that is the key to physical alchemy. The wise will understand what we say, the cheap organisms are not entitled to know anyhow. However, bear in mind that the alchemy of the soul is the first step, the alchemy of the body is the second, social alchemy is the third, while physical alchemy is the fourth and last step which is to be taken in our quest for absolute power.

The Hermetic Art

ON THOUGHT AND SENSE

That the Beautiful and Good Is in God Only and Elsewhere Nowhere

TEXT

Parthey (G.), *Hermetis Trismegisti Poemander* (Berlin, 1854), 60-67.

Patrizzi (F.), *Nova de Universis Philosophia* (Venice, 1593), 14-15.

Mead (G. R. S.), *Thrice Greatest Hermes* (London, 1906), Corpus Hermeticum IX (X).

1. I gave the Perfect Sermon (*Logos*) yesterday, Asclepius; to-day I think it right, as sequel thereunto, to go through point by point the Sermon about Sense.

Now sense and thought do seem to differ, in that the former has to do with matter, the latter has to do with substance. But unto me both seem to be at-one and not to differ —in men I mean. In other lives sense is a at-oned with nature, but in men thought.

Now mind doth differ just as much from thought as God from divinity. For that divinity by God doth come to be, and by mind thought, the sister of the word (*logos*) and instruments of one another. For neither doth the word (*logos*) find utterance without thought, nor is thought manifested without word.

2. So sense and thought both flow to-

gether into man, as though they were entwined with one another. For neither without sensing can one think, nor without
thinking sense.

But it is possible [they say] to think a
thing apart from sense, as those who fancy
sights in dreams. But unto me it seems that
both of these activities occur in dream-
sight, and sense doth pass out of the sleeping
to the waking state.

For man is separated into soul and body,
and only when the two sides of his sense
agree together, does utterance of its thought
conceived by mind take place.

3. For it is mind that doth conceive all
thoughts—good thoughts when it receives
the thoughts from God, their contraries
when [it receiveth them] from one of the
daimonials; no part of Cosmos being free of
daimon, who stealthily doth creep into the
daimon who's illumined by God's Light,
and sow in him the seed of its own energy.

And mind conceives the seed thus sown,
adultery, murder, parricide, [and] sacrilege,
impiety, [and] strangling, casting down
precipices, and all such other deeds as are
the work of evil daimones.

4. The seeds of God, 'tis true, are few,
but vast and fair, and good-virtue and self-
control, devotion. Devotion is God-gnosis;
and he who knoweth God, being filled with
all good things, thinks Godly thoughts and
not thoughts like the many [think].

For this cause they who Gnostic are,
please not the many, nor the many them.
They are thought mad and laughed at;
they're hated and despised, and sometimes
even put to death.

For we did say that bad must needs dwell
here on earth, where 'tis in its own place.
Its place is earth, and not Cosmos, as some
will sometimes say with impious tongue.

But he who is a devotee of God, will bear
with all—once he has sensed the Gnosis.
For such an one all things, e'en though they
be for others bad, are for him good; deliberately he doth refer them all unto the
Gnosis. And, thing most marvellous, 'tis
he alone who maketh bad things good.

5. But I return once more to the Discourse (*Logos*) on Sense. That sense doth
share with thought in man, doth constitute
him man. But 'tis not [every] man, as I
have said, who benefits by thought; for this
man is material, that other one substantial.

For the material man, as I have said, [con-
sorting] with the bad, doth have his seed of
thought from daimons; while the substantial
men [consorting] with the Good, are saved
by God.

Now God is Maker of all things, and in
His making, He maketh all [at last] like to
Himself; but they, while they're becoming
good by exercise of their activity, are unproductive things.

It is the working of the Cosmic Course

that maketh their becomings what they are,
befouling some of them with bad and others
of them making clean with good.

For Cosmos, too, Asclepius, possesseth
sense-and-thought peculiar to itself, not like
to that of man. It is not so manifold, but as
it were a better and a simpler one.

6. The single sense-and-thought of Cosmos is to make all things, and make them
back into itself again, as Organ of the Will
of God, so organized that it, receiving all
the seeds into itself from God, and keeping
them within itself, may make all manifest,
and then dissolving them, make them all new
again; and thus, like a Good Gardener of
Life, things that have been dissolved, it
taketh to itself, and giveth them renewal
once again.

There is no thing to which it gives not
life; but taking them all unto itself it makes
them live, and is at the same time the Place
of Life and its Creator.

7. Now bodies matter [-made] are in
diversity. Some are of earth, of water some,
some are of air, and some of fire.

But they are all composed; some are more
[composite], and some are simpler. The
heavier ones are more [composed], the
lighter less so.

It is the speed of the Cosmos' Course that
works the manifoldness of the kinds of
births. For being a most swift Breath, it
doth bestow their qualities on bodies together

with the One Pleroma—that of Life.

8.   God, then, is Sire of Cosmos; Cosmos, of [all] in Cosmos.   And Cosmos is God's Son; but things in Cosmos are by Cosmos.

And properly hath it been called Cosmos [Order]; for that it orders all with their diversity of birth, with its not leaving aught without its life, with the unweariedness of its activity, the speed of its necessity, the composition of its elements, and the order of its creatures.

The same, then, of necessity and of propriety should have the name of Order.

The sense-and-thought, then, of all lives doth come into them from without, inbreathed by what contains [them all]; whereas Cosmos receives them once for all together with its coming into being, and keeps them as a gift from God.

9.   But God is not, as some suppose, beyond the reach of sense-and-thought.   It is through superstition men thus impiously speak.

For all the things that are, Asclepius, all are in God, are brought by God to be, and do depend upon Him—both things that act through bodies, and things that through soul-substance make [other things] to move, and things that make things live by means of spirit, and things that take unto themselves the things that are worn out.

And rightly so; nay, I would rather say, He doth not *have* these things; but I speak forth the truth, He *is* them all Himself. He doth not *get* them from without, but *gives* them out [from Him].

This is God's sense-and-thought, ever to move all things. And never time shall be when e'en a whit of things that are shall cease; and when I say "a whit of things that are," I mean a whit of God. For things that are, God hath; nor aught [is there] without Him, nor is He without aught.

10. These things should seem to thee, Asclepius, if thou dost understand them, true; but if thou dost not understand, things not to be believed.

To understand is to believe, to not believe is not to understand.

My word (*logos*) doth go before [thee] to the truth. But mighty is the mind, and when it hath been led by word up to a certain point, it hath the power to come before [thee] to the truth.

And having thought o'er all these things, and found them consonant with those which have already been translated by the reason, it hath [e'en now] believed, and found its rest in that Fair Faith.

To those, then, who by God's [good aid] do understand the things that have been said [by us] above, they're credible; but unto those who understand them not, incredible.

Let so much, then, suffice on thought-and-sense.

LESSON VI

Thought and Sense

1. I gave the Perfect Sermon (*Logos*) yesterday, Asclepius; to-day I think it right, as sequel thereunto, to go through point by point the Sermon about Sense.

Now sense and thought do seem to differ, in that the former has to do with matter, the latter has to do with substance. But unto me both seem to be at-one and not to differ—in men I mean. In other lives sense is at-oned with nature, but in men thought.

Now mind doth differ just as much from thought as God doth from divinity. For that divinity by God doth come to be, and by mind thought, the sister of the word (*Logos*) and instruments of one another. For neither doth the word (*Logos*) find utterance without thought, nor is thought manifested without word.

1. I gave the Perfect Sermon (*Logos*) yesterday, Asclepius; to-day I think it right, as sequel thereunto, to go through point by by point the Sermon about Sense.

The introductory paragraph indicates that this sermon on sense is in the nature of a sequel to the perfect sermon. As the perfect sermon is a discourse on initiations and goes into the whole matter touching initiations, it logically follows that this sermon clears up certain points that are left out

in the discourse on initiations, and which are in
the nature of supplemental matter and more
esoteric matter than what is contained in the perfect sermon. And we will find this to be true,
because in the perfect sermon a great deal is said
about sense, but the true nature of sense is not there
defined. This sermon is therefore a sequel to the
perfect sermon, in which he goes through point by
point the sermon or discourse on the nature of
sense. Therefore we have a right to expect Hermes
to cover every possible point dealing with the
subject of sense, and in this we are not disap-
pointed.

Now sense and thought do seem to differ,
in that the former has to do with matter, the
latter has to do with substance. But unto
me both seem to be at-one and not to differ—
in men I mean. In other lives sense is at-
oned with nature, but in men thought.

We are here assured that the difference between
thought and sense is simply this, that sense has to
do with matter, thought has to do with substance.
In other words, they are both actions of the soul
in which an awareness of the Kosmos is obtained.
We become aware of material things and conditions through sense. We become aware of substantial things by thought. This will undoubtedly
dumfound a great many, for Hermes clearly indicates that the man whose consciousness is purely
material, who knows nothing but the material,
never had a thought in his life; that all his knowledge has come through sense. He has sensed
things but has never done any thinking. Doubt-
less Hermes would designate our friends the mate-
rialists as the mindless or at least as the thought-
less. The whole conception that he brings to our

attention is that all conception of matter is sensed, and our conceptions of substance are thought. Now if you will study the terminology of most people you will see that they agree with Hermes, that they have not any thought, that they do not know how to think, that they are absolutely mindless. They say, for instance, that there is no sense in such and such a statement, thinking that they mean that it is contrary to reason or to intelligence. They say that someone has no sense, that people are senseless, that such and such a statement is nonsense. Now it is ordinarily assumed that they mean by this to indicate absence of intelligence, but they cannot get by with that proposition. If a statement is nonsense it is contrary to sense not contrary to thought; if a man has no sense it indicates that his power of sense, his ability to sense material things and conditions is defective. If a statement has no sense in it, it is simply that it is not a statement of the testimony of the senses, that is to say it is contrary to material conditions. Common sense is whatever concept the senses of the people in general will give them of matter. It is also a common error to imagine that one can by thought ascertain material facts. Such a conception is absolutely erroneous. Thought has nothing to do with matter. All material conceptions come through sense, while all knowledge of substance comes through thought. If one does not believe that there is any such thing as immaterial substance it simply proves that he has never thought in his life; that his thinker has never been active; that it has been out of commission; that he has merely been sensing things. He further contends, however, that thought and sense in man are at-one and do not differ. By this he means that they act simultaneously; that is to say that they do not occupy separate fields or zones of consciousness so that one goes without the other, but rather he holds that sense and thought are interactive, each one having its influence upon the other. And this is quite characteristic of the absolute monism which is so common to Hermes; that is to say of his unwillingness to separate or divide the universe. He prefers to look at it as a whole. Therefore he does not conceive of substance as distinct from matter, or of matter as distinct from substance. They are not in his mind two things but rather give two phases of one verity. Therefore he merges thought and sense so far as man is concerned. In other lives, that is in the animals, sense is at-oned with nature. That is to say nature expresses itself through the sense of the animal. The animal senses nature but in man nature expresses itself through thought. In other words he would hold that one gets an understanding of things by the activity of his thought. Consequently it is evident that Hermes would not consider that there are very many men living today, he would argue that there are a lot of animals walking on their hind legs, but not many men. Because only he who conceives a thing by thought is in his concept human.

Now mind doth differ just as much from thought as God doth from divinity. For that divinity by God doth come to be, and by mind thought, the sister of the word (*Logos*) and instruments of one another. For neither doth the word (*Logos*) find utterance without thought, nor is thought manifested without word.

Hermes here draws the distinction between mind and thought. He illustrates the difference between mind and thought by the difference between God and divinity. He would argue that there would be no divinity if there was no God. God is what produces divinity; divinity is in the nature of the manifesting essence of God. God in action produces divinity. Divinity is therefore the activity of God; the product of God's action within Himself; the product of this, the character of God in a certain sense, is what we term divinity. Now in the same way, just as divinity comes to be as the result of the active life of God it follows that thought comes into being because of mind. Mind is therefore an active principle, a generative force, which becomes active in terms of thought. Thought must also be distinguished from thoughts, for thought is that process emanating from mind which tends to engender thoughts; thought therefore being the generative action of mind and thoughts the things generated.

Thought is the sister of the logos or word. Now the logos, the word, in this sense must not be confounded with the words which people speak that is, with articulate speech. It is rather the ideal form of the word. It is rather the tendency for thoughts to take a psychic form which when uttered becomes a word. The logos is therefore the psychic prototype or archetype of a word. And this is the sister of thought because thought becomes logic; that is, as we think, our thought naturally assumes the form of a psychic image, which in turn expresses itself as the uttered word, that is expresses itself through the medium of sound. They are mutually instruments, the one of the other. The logos or word does not find utterance without thought; in fact there would be no logos, no spirit of a word, were it not for thought giving utterance to this word. And thought can never be made manifest without the word. In other words, thought is in the unmanifest state until the word has been found. The word is what makes the thought manifest; words are therefore the means of concreting thought. We think, but cannot clarify, express or utter our thought, until the logos or the word is found through which such utterance becomes possible. This will throw a great deal of light upon the subject of the origin of language. In other words, there exists no word until after someone has believed the thing that that word expresses. Until we accept as true what the word expresses the word is not coined. Articulate speech is therefore the means of expressing the logos. The logos therefore when conceived out of thought causes someone to formulate an uttered word which will express it. The faculty of language is therefore the faculty for giving utterance by means of articulate speech to the logos which brings forth from our thought. The man who has thoughts which he cannot find words to express, whose thinking cannot be properly expressed, is an illustration of the principle of which we are speaking. This is the stage when thought has not expressed itself by means of the logos. It is in the shadow stage,—the man cannot definitely express his thought. This is the relation between thought, logos, and uttered speech, and this will give us a fair conception of the nature of thought and its relation to sense; always bearing in mind that thought relates itself to substance and not to matter. Therefore thoughts are not of the material but of the substantial. Therefore logoi, or words, are forms of the reason and reason is therefore the expression of mind, the vehicle of mind, just as logoi are the vehicles of expressed thoughts.

2. So sense and thought both flow together into man, as though they were entwined with one another. For neither without sensing can one think, nor without thinking sense.

But it is possible [they say] to think a thing apart from sense, as those who fancy sights in dreams. But unto me it seems that both of these activities occur in dreamsight, and sense doth pass out of the sleeping to the waking state.

For man is separated into soul and body, and only when the two sides of his sense agree together, does utterance of its thought conceived by mind take place.

So sense and thought both flow together into man, as though they were entwined with one another. For neither without sensing can one think, nor without thinking sense.

Sense and thought do not act separately upon man, but on the contrary, they are simultaneously active, and in fact blend into one composite force. They are mutually interactive at all times. Another point we must bear in mind is this, both sense and thought flow into man. By this we are to understand that both sense and thought are kosmical forces, existing independent of man, which flow into him, from without, and entering him, awaken sense and thought in him. He does not hold that they are original with man, but rather that man is the Organ through which, both sense and thought are made manifest. Hence, man is negative, while both sense and thought are positive forces in their action through man. The sense referred to here cannot therefore be confined to physical sensation, but must refer to something a great deal higher. Sensing is always accompanied by thought, and likewise is thought ever accompanied by sensing, the two are merely two aspects of the one process.

But it is possible [they say] to think a thing apart from sense, as those who fancy sight in dreams. But unto me it seems that both of these activities occur in dream-sight, and sense doth pass out of the sleeping to the waking state.

We are next lead into the question of thought independent of sense. He takes the position that there is no such thing. The error which he is here refuting is due to the other error that sense is confined to the physical sensations. This is wrong. Sense is in reality that power which brings one into contact with that which is exterior to him, and in this way, through contact, awakens the action of thought. Dream-sight is in reality more sensing than thought, though both activities are present. There is a continuity of the sense of the sleeping state into that of the waking state. Sense not being confined to the body, it transcends the plane of physical matter.

For man is separated into soul and body, and only when the two sides of his sense agree together, does utterance of its thought conceived by mind take place.

As man is separated into soul and body, it follows that there is a corresponding separation of sense, into soul sense and bodily sense. Thought is the result of the union of the soul sense with the sense of the body. In this way, is man's sensing made to include the soul world and the physical world. The physical and the Psychic are therefore both matters of sense. Through the dual sense, there is deposited in man the germ of thought, which is conceived in the mind, very much after the manner of the conception of a child in the womb of the mother, so that the mind acting as the matrix in which sense is deposited, becomes in this way, fecundated by sense, and as a result, thought is conceived within the mind, from whence it is born into consciousness. This will give to us a true conception of the nature of sense and thought. The basis of all sensing is the Kosmic Sense. This sense, being sensible of all things in Kosmos, acts upon both soul and body, with the result that it acts upon both the body and soul in such a manner as to there deposit this sense, causing us to become aware of that sense, though as a feeling, and not as a mental conception. This sensing acts upon the mind, so that, being acted upon by the dynamic motion of sense, it moves in such a manner as to conceive thought. Sense in man, is therefore the process of Kosmic Sense acting upon him in such a way as to make him sensible of that which is held in Kosmic Sense. This process, acting upon the mind, causes it to conceive the thought, corresponding to that which has been sensed, which is in that manner born into consciousness. This will show that the conception of thought is only possible in a mind fecundated by sense, and that this fecundation by sense is the result of the Kosmic Sense contacting the Soul as well as the body. It will therefore follow that the mind can conceive no thoughts which are not the reflex of corresponding sensings. This leads us to the conclusion that the first requisite is not so much a matter of mental power as it is one of sensing. Mentality therefore does not depend upon brain capacity or intellectual culture half so much as upon a soul and body, so sensitively attuned that they will respond to the vibration of Kosmic Sense. The first requisite is to be very sensitive, so that we will respond to, and register all possible aspects of Kosmic Sense. This ability will definitely limit the extent of the mental operations, though of course the mental operations may not come up to the full extent of the sensing capacity. This will depend upon the possession of a mind capable of acting under all the impulses of sense, in such a manner as to conceive thought under each one of them. This will depend upon the sensitiveness and upon the responsiveness and activity of the mind. Mind is therefore the feminine womb into which sense deposits the germs of thought. Sensing is the fecundating action which fecundates the mind with the seeds of future thoughts, while Kosmic Sense is the fecundator of all minds. From this point of view the nature of man, is essentially feminine.

We have here a very important lesson in the Hermetic Art. The source of all things must be found in nature, we can originate nothing, but must merely duplicate the work of nature, though we can improve upon this under certain limitations. But we must derive the Seed from nature. The first thing is, therefore, to prepare a suitable receptacle in which the work is to be performed. After this we must deposit in this receptacle a suitable matter as the Matrix in which conception is to take place. After this, we must have a transmissive element through which motion can be imparted to this plastic mass, and the last step is to have the active principle of the universe brought into direct contact with the transmissive agent. If all these elements are properly prepared we will find that the Seed will be deposited from the Kosmos into our receptacle and in this way will be developed into actuality after the manner of the conception of thought in the mind. However, do not make this mistake, do not imagine that you can make either Gold, or Life. Life can never be created, though we can direct the form of the evolution through which it passes. Gold is never made, it is born. We must learn to conceive it in the Vase of

Art, exactly as thought is conceived in the mind of man. Remember this, the Seed of Gold is in the Kosmos, it must fecundate the First Matter and in this way, conceive gold in the Vase of Art. This is the Alchemist's Secret.

LESSON VII

The Conception of Thought

3.   For it is mind that doth conceive of thoughts—good thoughts when it receives the seeds from God, their contraries when [it receiveth them] from one of the daimonials; no part of Cosmos being free of daimons, who stealthily doth creep unto the daimon who's illumined by God's Light, and sow in him the seed of its own energy.

And mind conceives the seed thus sown; adultery, murder, parricide, [and] sacrilege, impiety, [and] strangling, casting down precipices, and all such other deeds as are the work of evil daimons.

For it is mind that doth conceive of thoughts—good thoughts when it receives the seeds from God, their contraries when [it receiveth them] from one of the daimonials; no part of Cosmos being free of daimons, who stealthily doth creep into the daimon who's illumined by God's Light, and sow in him the seed of its own energy.

All thoughts are conceived in mind, conceived from seed sown in the mind from some source external to the mind itself. This must necessarily be true because it is through sense that the seeds are sown in mind. After being deposited in mind these seeds go through a process of transformation, —or rather they stimulate the mind to action resulting in the conception of corresponding thoughts. If the mind receives the seed of thought from God it must conceive good thoughts, that is corresponding in a measure to the nature of God, because thought which is conceived as a result of the seed must correspond to the seed antecedent to the conception. While just the contrary is the result when the mind receives the seed from one of the daimonials. Inasmuch as the character of the daimonials is not good but the reverse, it follows therefore that the seed emanating from the daimonial must be a daimonial seed, that is to say a seed partaking of the nature of the daimons, and this daimonial seed has started into operation by the specific action of the mind, it must necessarily follow that the mind will conceive daimonial thoughts; evil thoughts; thoughts partaking of the nature of the daimons. No part of Kosmos is free of daimons; that is to say there is no part of the Kosmos that is not occupied by daimons, the daimonial hosts being so numerous, so extensive, that every part of the Kosmos is inhabited by them; hence there are always daimons present to deposit the seeds of evil thought within the mind of each and every one. These evil thoughts must be conceived in the minds of all unless the soul has reached such a degree of refinement and spiritualization that it is positive to the daimons and negative only to God. This is really the only guarantee anyone has,—his spiritual thought, which will establish the right degree of polarity. Now we find here a very important point brought out and at the same time one that very few realize, and that is this, no man ever thinks thoughts which are entirely dependent upon his own mentality; all thoughts are conceived in the mind from seed sown in the mind by beings external to that mind. Either God or the daimons, using God here in the sense not only of the One and-only-one but also in the sense of the gods as well. Deity sows good seed in the mind, the daimonials sow evil seed, and all our thinking is the result of a mind fecundated by the seeds of divinity or of the daimons. A mind unfecundated by such seed is incapable of conceiving thought.

We are informed that these daimons stealthily creep into the daimon who is illumined by God's Light. We must bear in mind that according to Hermes the daimons are not only those kosmic powers or beings, but he also terms the soul of man a daimon. It is the daimon in man. Now we must bear in mind that the daimons are an order of beings subordinate to the gods, because of their creative power the same term is applied to the human soul, which is also creative. The daimon in man is his soul; the daimon illumined by God's light means a higher order of soul than what we mean when we ordinarily speak of the soul of man. It means the soul into which the light of God has shined, and thus the soul being illumined by a higher degree of enlightenment than what is common to the grasp of the human understanding. God's light must not be confounded with God himself. Light is one of the rays emanating from God. Now this emanating ray of the divine light has shone into the soul of man and quickened his intelligence, so that it is thereby illumined by this light. He is the daimon that is illumined by God's light mentioned here. Now we are informed that these daimons stealthily creep into the daimon illumined by God's light and sow in him the seed of their own energy. In other words, although one has reached that stage of development where his soul is illumined by the light of God he is not yet safe from demonial interference. He may be inspired, or illumined; the light of God may shine into his soul and thus give him an illuminated vision of eternal things, nevertheless this does not prevent the daimons from creeping in and sowing in the soul also the seed of their own energy, so that the energy of the daimons will cause the awakening of activity which will in this way sow seed into the mind causing daimonial thought to be there conceived and manifested in act.   Therefore we can see that in reality man does little or nothing. The teaching that man's life is in the hands of fate is really true, because man cannot think of himself, he can only conceive in the mind such thoughts as the seeds sown in his mind by God, or the daimons, will inspire, unless, of course, it be the thought that is awakened by the senses and by experience and observation, etc. But we are here speaking of the higher thought.   And this is the real key to dual inspiration,—thought of the gods and thought of the daimons. All daimonial inspiration will necessarily lead to evil thought and evil deeds, while the inspiriation on the part of the gods will likewise inevitably lead to good thoughts and good deeds. Therefore the evil in man is really the result of his responsiveness to daimonial impulses.

And mind conceives the seed thus sown; adultery, murder, parricide [and] sacrilege, impiety, [and] strangling, casting down precipices, and all such other deeds as are the work of evil daimons.

The seeds of the demonial energy being sown in the mind by acting upon the substance of the mind causes it to conceive the seed thus sown; in other words, thoughts corresponding to those seeds, that is to say, daimonial thoughts, are conceived and these thoughts breed emotions and the emotions actions, and thus adultery, murder, parricide, sacrilege, impiety and all such kindred evil deeds, are the result of the seeds of daimons entering into the mind and there conceiving thought or causing the mind to conceive thought which engenders action. Thus sins are not due to the total depravity of man; they are not due to inbred sin from generation to generation; such superstitions are without foundation in fact. Sins are due to the fact that the energy of the daimons enters into man's mind and entering there deposits the seed which conceives corresponding thought and ultimately engenders evil deeds. Man is responsible only to the extent that his mind is receptive to the seeds of the demonial energy. To that extent he is responsible. In other words, he is responsible to the extent that he is not perfectly divine, to the extent that any influence other than the thought of God can operate. We have here a very important doctrine; a doctrine which the cheap organisms seem absolutely unable to grasp; namely, that morality is of very little importance; that the really important thing is the spiritual state of the soul; that everything depends not upon specific deeds, but upon the degree of refinement in spirituality of the human soul. When we come to realize this we will pay little attention to what a man says or does; we will be more interested in the scale of humanity to which he belongs. Man is really to be classified by the degree in which he has approached the divine, the degree of fineness in the mind. In other words, there are no such things as good men or bad men, if you will look at it properly, but there is such a thing as inferior and superior types of man. Man must be graded that way, not in the ordinary way that is common to the cheap organisms. In other words, cheap organisms are incapable of anything but evil, while superior organisms in proportion to the relative degree of their superiority, evolve the capacity for good.

4. The seeds of God 'tis true, are few, but vast and fair, and good—virtue and self-control, devotion. Devotion is God-Gnosis; and he who knoweth God being filled with all good things, thinks godly thoughts and not thoughts like the many [think].

For this cause they who Gnostic are, please not the many nor the many them. They are thought mad and laughed at; they're hated and despised, and sometimes even put to death.

For we did say that bad must needs dwell here on earth, where 'tis in its own place. Its place is earth, and not Cosmos as some will sometimes say with impious tongue.

But he who is a devotee of God, will bear with all once he has sensed the Gnosis. For such an one all things, e'en though they be for others bad, are for him good; deliberately he doth refer them all unto the Gnosis and, thing most marvelous, 'tis he alone who maketh bad things good.

The seeds of God 'tis true, are few, but vast and fair, and good—virtue and self-control, devotion. Devotion is God-Gnosis; and he who knoweth God, being filled with all good things, thinks godly thoughts and not thoughts like the many [think].

Having shown the nature of the seeds of the daimons, their effect upon the thinking and life of man, he next turns his attention to the seeds of God. These seeds of God, that is the seeds which are able to emanate from God and entering the mind of man conceive thoughts after their kind, are few, but they are vast and fair, and good; because nothing could be vaster, nothing could be fairer, nothing could be better than the seeds emanating directly from God. We might say there are three characteristics that are conceived in the mind of man as a result of the divine seed and they come only from the divine seed. These are virtue, self-control and devotion. It must be borne in mind that virtue was used in ancient times in an entirely different sense to what it is used at the present time. It was synonymous with virile manhood, with all those characteristics which, as the fellow said, are characteristics of a "shore-enough man." It was not virtuous to do things which would not be manly. A man might have no religious scruples about a thing, but he was too virtuous to do it, that is, it would be beneath his dignity as a "shore-enough man" to do anything of the kind. Virtue, therefore, represents the manly quality, the proud manly quality that scorns to do that which is mean or low, that which is not characteristic of the ideal man. And this virtue can only operate in the mind of a man as the result of his receiving divine seeds in his mind. This seed of virtue emanating from divinity, that is from the anthropos, the archetypal divine man, when that seed enters the human mind it conceives virtuous thoughts, thoughts proper to a real man; the manly thoughts, virtuous thoughts, and all virtuous actions emanate from this virtuous thinking. Now bear this in mind, there is none of the humble, worm-of-the-dust, poor cringing sinner, in the virtuous man. A timid man, a meek man in the ordinary sense of the word, can never have any virtue. A virtuous man is always proud, he always covers the ground he stands on, he is sure of himself, absolutely conscious of himself—of his worth. He knows his greatness, therefore he must be proud as the eagle if he expects to be virtuous.

The next divine seed is that of self-control. It is this which gives man the self-contained, self-mastering attitude. That is to say, man is not carried away by his passions, by his impressions, by his impulses; but he dominates them all, he controls them; all the aspects of his manifest selfhood are in leash, they are under perfect control. Such a man can say truly I am the *Yauwa;* I am the I-will-be-what-I-will-be. In other words, it is this quality of self-control that makes the superman. And this comes from its divine source. It is the proud self-controlled, self-restrained impulses that develop corresponding thought and that enable man through reason to subjugate all his passions and using them, but not allowing them to use him. The self-controlled man is not a man without passions; he is not an eastern acetic who subdues or crushes out his passions; he is full of passion, but it is always under the rigid control of his will directed by his intelligence, so that he can make use of those passions when he needs them in his business, but never lets them interfere with him.

The other seed of God is devotion. This seed that is implanted in the mind of man is the tendency to draw his soul out to God. It, when deposited in the mind, conceives thoughts which naturally turn to God, which are drawn to God as the steel to the magnet. The God power is the magnetism which attracts such devotional thoughts toward God, hence devotion is in reality a yearning after God, a taking hold upon God, and we are informed that such devotion is God-Gnosis; in other words, the Gnosis, or knowledge of God, comes by reason of a mind that turns in the direction of God; in other words, a mind is never able to learn anything about God until it becomes interested in the subject; until God becomes a very attractive subject for our mental contemplation we can know nothing about God. Now devotion does not mean mumbling prayers, it does not mean the acts of devotion which fanatics think it means; it means a mental interest in God, a yearning for the knowledge of God, for an understanding of the essence of God. It is this devotion, therefore, this turning of the mind toward God, which is itself the outgrowth of the seeds of God being planted there, which gives man Gnosis of God. He who knows God as a result of this God-Gnosis operating in his mind is filled with all good things. That is to say, the Gnosis of God in the mind renders it negative to all the seeds emanating from on high, all the non-demonial seeds, and thus they enter into the mind and soul, hence the seeds of all things good are there and the conception of those good things begins. He thinks godly thoughts and not thoughts like the many think. In other words, the thinking of this one being conceived of seed emanating from God, is godly, godlike, or similar to the thinking of God the Mind, or of the lesser divinities. It is thinking after the nature of God's thought and hence, of course, it is not like the many think at all, because the many have their thinking conceived from daimonial seed. The result is the Gnosis is in time entirely immune from the seed emanating from the daimonial because he has a mind completely filled with the seed of God; all his thinking is controlled by them and consequently there is no unoccupied area in his mind, no part of the mind that might be acted upon by the seed of daimons, hence no thought other than God thought can be conceived therein.

For this cause they who Gnostic are,

please not the many nor the many them. They are thought mad and laughed at; they're hated and despised and sometimes even put to death.

In this paragraph Hermes explains to us the antipathy between the Gnostic and the cheap organism. There is no greater fallacy than the idea that a good man will win the love of a bad man,— win the love of everybody; there is no greater tommy-rot than this nonsensical proposition. The cheap organism hates the enlightened soul beyond anyone in all the world. There is the most intense antipathy on the part of the rabble toward the superior man. If one finds himself hated and despised by the people, let him rest assured they are paying him the highest compliment. They are incapable of appreciating the attitude of the good, the pure, the spiritual. It is not only a lack of appreciation, it is an attitude of absolute antagonism, absolute antipathy. And why? Because the rabble thinks only such thoughts as are conceived from seed entering their minds from the daimons, while the Gnostic thinks only such thoughts as are conceived by seed entering the mind from God. The result is that the same antipathy that exists between God and the daimons must exist between the Gnostic and the cheap organism. And this is not to be deplored altogether, because they have separate and distinct functions. The cheap organism is related to matter, the Gnostic, on the other hand, is related to substance. The cheap organism, the material man or the daimonial man measuring everything by his own ignorance, thinks the Gnostic is mad and laughs at him. Because of the Gnostic's indifference to matter and the cheap organism's indifference to substance, they are hated and despised as weak, as inferior, and are sometimes even put to death because of their superior knowledge. They can never please the cheap organism, and the cheap organism can never please them. Any man who talks about loving everybody is either a deliberate liar or else he has no spiritual realization. The Gnostic may tolerate the cheap organism, in fact, he should, but to be pleased with him is simply out of the question. It is utterly impossible for the developed soul to take pleasure in, to enjoy the society, of cheap organisms. Because they are as far asunder as the poles, they represent two separate and distinct extremes of existence, and this accounts for the persecution of the pure and holy by the cheap organisms. They want to get rid of them because of this antipathy, and in the last analysis, the real thing that is involved, is the war of the daimons to keep the gods from gaining influence on earth.

For we did say that bad must needs dwell here on earth, where 'tis in its own place. Its place is earth, and not Cosmos as some will some times say with impious tongue.

Here we have the crux of the situation. The earth is the realm of bad, bad must needs dwell here on earth where it is in its own place. The earth is therefore the place of bad; the space in which the bad is made manifest. The evolution on the earth for the present time at least must be through the bad. All terrene evolution is due to the operation of bad principles. This is not true of the Kosmos, but it is true of the earth. Now as the earth must evolve through the bad, therefore it must evolve through the action of the daimons. They are the ones who conduct the terrene evolution. Hence this evolution depends upon the proportion of bad that is manifested here,—that is the daimonial influence. Now in order that man as a race may evolve, that the earth may go through its terrene experience, speaking from the standpoint of race, he must be a bad man, and therefore he will express in his thought the seed of the daimon. The result is the kosmic man, that is one functioning in Kosmos as well as in the earth, a substantial man, a good man, is a disruptive influence in the life of the earth. In other words, he is a heavy charge of nitro-glycerine, lyddite and gun cotton dropped into the social fabric. He is always more or less of a disruptive influence. And that is really his purpose. It is not intended in the kosmic scheme that there should be very many good men on the earth. It is after the manner of an aerolite, a comet, or a meteor, descending from heaven to knock the earth back into shape, or to shake and disorganize its crystalized state, so that it will go through an additional ferment as it were. Naturally the daimons and the daimonial men do not appreciate the value of such disturbing influences. This being the case, they show a considerable measure of opposition to such visitations from the heavenly world, and this is the real cause of the antipathy which the daimonial man or the cheap organism bears to the Gnostic, or the superman. Kosmos is not the sphere of evil, of bad, as is the earth, but is relatively good; hence the substantial man is a relatively good man. Of course there is no such thing as an absolutely good man; but the kosmic man is relatively good, and his goodness makes him a menace to the stability of terrene society.

But he who is a devotee of God, will bear with all once he has sensed the Gnosis. For such an one all things, e'en though they be for others bad, are for him good; deliberately he doth refer them all unto the Gnosis, and, thing most marvelous, 'tis he alone who maketh bad things good.

The man in whom the God seed of devotion has been sown, so that his thinking becomes devotional, causing his whole mind to turn in the direction of God, so that he becomes a devotee of God, one devoted to God, one whose business or avocation in life is service to God, this attitude will cause him to bear with bad if he has once sensed the Gnosis. Now notice, the Gnosis comes through sense. That is to say, Gnosis is not acquired by man's mental striving. Gnosis is sown in the mind of man, which acts as a receptacle for its being deposited there when that man has attained devotion. Devotion brings him into that state of close contact with God which illumines his mind with the light of Gnosis, causing it to conceive thoughts under the impulse of the divine light. Such an one will bear with all. For such an one all things, even though for others bad, are for him good. He deliberately refers them all unto the Gnosis. In other words, the Gnostic is so wise that he realizes every bad thing serves a good purpose. He realizes that all evil is good in the making. That is to say that good is bound to come out of bad, of evil; that the bad is absolutely necessary for the evolution of matter; hence he knows that the cheap organisms who are poking fun at him will be Gnostics just like him in the course of about thirty thousand years, and he knows that they would not be Gnostics then if they were not bad men now. He knows that this very bad principle is the principle of terrene evolution, that matter can be evolved in no other way; therefore he realizes that the bad man is a man who can only evolve through being bad, consequently he does not condemn the bad

man, he does not hate him, he simply realizes
that the bad man by being bad and as
mean as he can be is doing the very best he
can under the circumstances, and that such
bad people are absolutely necessary for the work
in the world, for the material progress of the
world. That is another thing that we must bear
in mind. The principal function of man at the
present stage of evolution is the cultivation and
exploitation of the earth; the development of nature; this is his principal function. But if he had
any sense he would not do it, he would not waste
his valuable time on such things. Consequently
it is very fortunate that the vast majority of the
human family is evil; because they are here to
subdue the earth, to harness the physical powers
of the earth; yet such work will only be performed
by one who does not see into the substantial realm;
consequently all this bad serves a wonderfully good
purpose; it serves to transform all matter. So the
Gnostic deliberately refers them all unto the
Gnosis. That is to say, he looks at these processes
of bad, and these bad people from the standpoint
of the light, which the Gnosis throws upon the subject. He realizes that the man is a workman who
is doing some particular work, and from the standpoint of the Gnosis we are able to see the relation
which that particular work will bear to the fin-
ished product. The most marvelous thing of all
is that it is the Gnostic alone who makes all things
good. Here we have the subtle alchemy of the
Gnostic life, that mental alchemy which causes the
Gnostic to see the bad as good by seeing that it is
but the crude form of a good condition that is
going to be brought about by and by; by seeing
that it is a stage in the transaction and looking at
it as though it had accomplished that, seeing the
end from the beginning, as it were; looking at
everything not as a thing in itself, but as a part of

the sequence, a stage in the course of development. Therefore all things are good to him because they are steps in the process which is bound to turn out good in the end. Therefore to the Gnostic all is good. And here we are able to see where the Gnostic rises superior to all other men. He knows that the end justifies the means, because the means is always for the sake of the realization of the end, that is all that things exist for. Consequently he may do things which to others would be very bad but to him they are perfectly good. Things that would be criminal and sinful in the cheap organism, are quite virtuous and proper in a Gnostic, because the Gnostic does all he does as a means of realizing the good; therefore through the application of his wisdom and understanding which he has due to his superior unfoldment, he is able to take all evil conditions and transmute them into good influences, by using them as a means of realizing the good. Hence the Gnostic is above good and evil, the categories of right and wrong have no existence for him, seeing that he is the soldier of truth and right in the absolute. Consequently whatever he does is right. The Gnostic can do no wrong. Therefore the world hates the Gnostic, who is above their moral code. The one who stands so high that nothing that he can do can fail to be better than the best that is done by anyone else is a menace to the liberty of the host of cheap organisms because he stands above them in every sense of the word. His alchemy is one of mind, one of thought, of intelligent direction. He is able through the power of his will to cause influences which otherwise would work for evil, to attain to the realization of the highest good. Thus the Gnostic is the great alchemist of the mind and at the same time is he the projectile that explodes and disintegrates the shams of society, scattering to the four winds the crystallized forms. Thus by disrupting them he forces them to again find adjustment. This is the true function of the Gnostic, the alchemist of the mind.

LESSON VIII

The Kosmic Course

5. But I return once more to the Discourse (*Logos*) on Sense. That sense doth share with thought in man, doth constitute him man. But 'tis not [every] man, as I have said, who benefits by thought; for this man is material, that other one substantial.

For the material man, as I have said, [consorting] with the bad, doth have his seed of thought from daimons; while the substantial men [consorting] with the Good, are saved by God.

Now God is Maker of all things, and in His making, He maketh all [at last] like to Himself; but they, while they're becoming good by exercise of their activity, are unproductive things.

It is the working of the Cosmic Course that maketh their becomings what they are, befouling some of them with bad and others of them making clean with good.

For Cosmos, too, Asclepius, possesseth sense-and-thought peculiar to itself, not like to that of man; 'tis not so manifold, but as it were a better and a simpler one.

But I return once more to the Discourse (*Logos*) on Sense. That sense doth share with thought in man, doth constitute him man. But 'tis not [every] man, as I have said, who benefits by thought; for this man is material, that other one substantial.

The sharing of sense and thought, that is the mutual interrelation of sense and thought in the conception of consciousness, is what constitutes the human nature. Without this combination, man would not be man, but merely one of the animal creation. The distinction between the two is in this, in the animals, sense causes the universe or nature to impress itself directly upon the animal. This direct impression of nature upon the animal through sense, constitutes what we call instinct, hence the actions of the animal are instinctive and impulsive. In man, sense acts through the medium of thought, awakening corresponding thoughts, and these enter the consciousness, and hence, instead of man having an instinctive sense of nature, he forms an intelligent concept of nature. It is this intelligent rather than instinctive action which distinguishes man as man and not as animal. At the same time we must bear in mind that all men are not benefitted by thought. There are two distinct classes of men, material men and substantial men. As thought is related to substance, it will follow that the material man is unable to do any real thinking. To grasp this, we must understand the nature of the thinking process. While it is true that it is the action of sense upon the mind that causes the conception of thought, but at the same time it will never do to assume that a thought is merely a picture of an object photographed upon the mind by sense. The thought is conceived in the mind, and is therefore composed of the substance of the mind itself. The thought is therefore, in the order of a substantial correspondent of the thing sensed, and hence it is related to the substantial operation back of the thing sensed, it is hence much more accurate than is sense. The function of sense then, is to get at the forms of things, while the function of thought is to get at their essences. Now, if man is substantial, his most active part is the soul, which being substantial and not material, will give ample opportunity for the conception of thought, while if one is material, his body being the most important and active portion of his being, there will be little opportunity for the conception of thought, and this being the case, in the material man thought does little more than to perpetuate the images presented through sense. Thus the material man has not the benefit of the mental quintessence of sense, which constitutes true thought, and which is the principle characteristic of the substantial man. Even when thought is in a measure present in the material man, it does not elevate him as it does the substantial man, for his thought being material and not substantial, he has no conception of the substance of things.

For the material man, as I have said, [consorting] with the bad, doth have his seed of thought from daimons; while the substantial men [consorting] with the Good, are saved by God.

The material man can have no thought of anything other than the earth life and experience. To him the material is the all. To him, facts are all that there are, hence his consciousness is filled up with material facts. As these relate to the bad alone, he has no concept of the substantial or the good, and thus, thinking only of the bad, that is, of the material, the mind is polarized entirely with the daimons. A mind which recognizes only the material, soon leads to a character that is completely material even in its aspirations. Such an one, failing to realize that there is any thing other than the material, naturally comes to the point where he seeks for the material as the one thing needful. This causes such an one to choose the material realm, which is under the control of the daimons, and of course subjects him to them. This being the case, all the seed of his thought is from the daimons, and thus, his thought is purely daimonial in as much as the seed which conceives all his thoughts are of daimonial origin. On the other hand, the substantial man, functioning in the soul, sees the substantial rather than the material. This leads him to a metaphysical view of nature, which causes him to live in a world of ideas rather than in one of facts. This enables him to function in the higher regions of Kosmos, leading a life in which the consciousness is largely substantial. As a result, he becomes largely indifferent to material things, and in proportion the substantial becomes more and more important. In the course of time, he comes to see in the ideal the one thing needful. Having become indifferent to the material, the bad, he of course becomes the more attached to the substantial and hence to the Good. This leads him into a state of polarity with the Good, with the result that his mind being closed to the seed of the daimons, it is now open to the seed of God, hence all his seed of thought is derived from God. This causes him to think in the divine manner, and hence he is saved by God, that is, the seed of God, conceives in the mind, kindred thoughts, so that his mind is completely closed to the seed of the daimons. He is thus saved from the influence of the daimons, by having his mind under the control of God.

Now God is Maker of all things, and in

His making, He maketh all [at last] like to Himself; but they, while they're becoming good by exercise of their activity, are unproductive things.

God is the maker of everything. Nothing comes into being, save that which He has made. As all things are the result of the Ideas of God, it follows that their real being is in the divine idea that originated them. They subsist in the divine mind at a time anterior to that during which they exist out of it. Living in the Divine Idea at first they are divine, and, while they are degraded through their course of mutation in Kosmos, they are nevertheless destined in the end to attain that Ideal Divinity which was theirs in the beginning. Before they can reach that state, they must pass through a period of evolution in Kosmos, during which time they will purge out the bad from their composition, and ultimately attain the status of the good. It is through the exercise of their activity that all bad things become good. Goodness is therefore, merely the result of growth in the bad things. During this time, however, they can produce nothing. The production of anything will mean their ceasing to become good for the time being at least. They are merely evolving themselves into the good state.

It is the working of the Cosmic Course that maketh their becomings what they are, befouling some of them with bad and others of them making clean with good.

The working of the Kosmic Course has for its purpose the perfecting and evolution of the Kosmos as a whole. It is not concerned with the effect of its evolutions upon any thing in particular, save as they effect the evolution of the Kosmos as a whole.   To this end, some things relatively good, that is, substantial, are degraded into material forms, and in that way befouled with bad, in a word, manifesting the bad quality of matter. At the same time, other things which are bad, owing to the fact that they are in material form, are purged of their materiality, and hence of their badness, and are made clean and good.   In this way, we are able to see the process of transmutation which is ever going on, the bad being transmuted into good, and in like manner the good being ever transmuted into bad.   It must be borne in mind that the purpose of the Kosmic Course is the perfection of all things as an unit, and hence the fate of a particular thing is of no moment, except as its fate effects the work of the Kosmic Course.   As the bad, that is the material, is transmuted into the good, that is the substantial, it tends to effect the status of matter in general, causing it to be gradually transformed until it approaches nearer and nearer to the substantial state.   In like manner, when the good, or substantial is driven into the bad or material state, it carries with it a considerable measure of the energy of the substantial condition, which being imprisoned in matter, seeks to return to the substantial condition. This energy, in its efforts to escape from the bond of matter, acts upon the matter holding it, in such a manner as to gradually transform it, and thus matter is in process of transmutation in the direction of the substantial condition.   The result is, the working of the Kosmic Course, while it is detrimental to the well being of the things themselves as they are befouled with bad, nevertheless, it tends to the substantialization of matter and the transmutation of the bad into the condition of the good. The Kosmic Course is therefore, nothing other than the course of the Alchemicalization of matter, and all things, have their place in that process of transmutation. Kosmos is the great Alchemist, and the status of every thing is but the temporary condition resulting from the process of Kosmic Transmutation. Thus, while all things are good in the beginning, and will be good in the end, each thing passes through a process of becoming bad, abides in a state of badness, and passes through a process of becoming good again, as a result of the effect which the Kosmic Course has upon it. Badness is therefore a state of development which every thing must go through. The purpose of which is the spiritualization of matter and the final elimination of bad from existence. All things, no matter how bad are therefore, doing their part in the deliverance of the universe from the rule of bad. We may draw from this a practical lesson, man should above all things avoid being too good. That is to say, one should avoid becoming so good that he is good for nothing. Remember, your function is to spiritualize the material world, not to be a pure spirit. This being the case, avoid becoming so spiritual that you can have no possible influence upon matter. If you do this, you will be of no earthly use, and the sooner you die and go to heaven, where you belong, the better. We have no use for Saints in this world, what we require is real live, red blooded men and women. Men and women who are not too spiritual to fight, to struggle and to do their part in the spiritualization of matter and hence in the regeneration of the universe. The saints all belong in heaven, what we want on earth is men. In other words, every one must be a Alchemist in his own proper field, small as it may be. This is the true function of all life, Alchemicalization, and above all, is it the work of man to transmute matter, and bring it a little closer to the spiritual status. In other words, the type of men that are most needed in the world are Hermetic Artists. Your work is not to prepare for heaven but to stay on the earth, and transmute it into the heavenly state, and stay on the job until it is done.

For Cosmos, too, Asclepius, possesseth sense-and-thought peculiar to itself, not like to that of man, 'tis not so manifold, but as it were a better and a simpler one.

Sense-and-thought are not confined to man, but are common to the Kosmos as well, the sense-and-thought of the Kosmos is one peculiar to the Kosmos, we do not find the like of it anywhere else. It is this sense-and-thought of the Kosmos that directs all the Kosmic operations. It is not so manifold as in the case of man, seeing that its functions are not so numerous, it is a simpler sense-and-thought and at the same time, a more powerful one, and one that operates on a more efficient plan. This sense-and-thought of the Kosmos is the principle that causes Kosmos to evolve in its own way, and by reason of its own power, and quite independent of any direction whatsoever. For this cause, Kosmos is alive, surcharged with its own sense, made intelligent by reason of its own thought, and animated by its own life.

6. The single sense-and-thought of Cosmos is to make all things, and make them back into itself again, as Organ of the Will of God, so organized that it, receiving all the seeds into itself from God, and keeping them within itself, may make all manifest, and [then] dissolving them, make them all new again; and thus, like a Good Gardener

of Life, things that have been dissolved, it
taketh to itself, and giveth them renewal
once again.

There is no thing to which it gives not
life; but taking all unto itself it makes them
live, and is at the same time the Place of
Life and its Creator.

Kosmos is Organ of the Will of God. It is the
vast space and substance into which the Will of
God, that is, the Dynamic Energy of the Ultimate
Deity enters, and moves therein. All the operations of the Will of God are through the medium
of this Kosmic Substance, which therefore becomes
the Substantial Organ through which the Divine
Will Force functions. This Kosmos is so organized that all the seeds from God, that is all the
Divine Ideas and the Monads engendered by them
in the Matrix of Ku, are driven forth into Kosmos
and are there deposited. They are all received
into Kosmos, after the manner of seeds being deposited in the earth in planting. They are retained
there by Kosmos. The single sense-and-thought of
Kosmos is to receive these seeds from God, which
it does by reason of its negative contact with God.
These seeds of God, when deposited in Kosmos,
cause it to conceive after their likeness, so that for
every seed coming from God, there is something
corresponding to it, conceived in Kosmos. In this
way it is the sense-and-thought of Kosmos to make
all things. It also makes all things back into itself
again, for nothing made by Kosmos is of perma-
ment form, seeing that all its making is with reference to itself. At the same time the tendency
engendered by the seed of God is permanent, and
hence this process is repeated unto infinity, and
this is the true basis of the Law of Karma. It

makes all things manifest, and then, when they
have become completely manifested, they are dissolved into Kosmos once more, and are again made
new again. Thus we have the perpetual reincarnation of every thing that is ever manifested in
Kosmos. It is through the endless sequence of
manifestations in form, and dissolutions of form
that the life contained in the form may manifest
yet again, that the things made in Kosmos are
going through an endless sequence of improve-
ment. Thus as the Gardener of Life, all things
that have been dissolved, are taken to Kosmos and
in the course of time made new again. Kosmos is
then, at once the Garden and the Gardener of Life
in all of its manifold forms. This direction of
this Process is the true nature of Kosmic Sense and
Kosmic Thought working as one process. Kosmic
Sense draws all the seeds of God into itself, and
likewise, draws into itself all things manifested,
dissolving them into its own substance. Kosmic
Thought directs the manifestation of all the seeds
of God, and likewise the renewal again of all
things dissolved. This is the single sense-and-
thought of Kosmos.

**There is no thing to which it gives not
life, but taking all unto itself it makes them
live, and is at the same time the Place of Life
and its Creator.**

All living things derive their life from Kosmos,
there is no life from any other source. It takes
every thing unto itself, and taking them unto itself,
it gives them life and makes them live. Death
merely means that a thing which has exhausted its
life force, is indrawn into Kosmos that it may be
given another lease of life. It is at the same time
the Place of Life and its Creator. It is the Place
of Life because it is the space in which all life

is made manifest, and in which all things are given
their life. All the seeds of life are deposited in
this space, and there are given the forms through
which they may manifest their life. All forms are
indrawn into it, that they may again be made to
live. It is likewise the Creator of Life, because
it is through the operation of Kosmos under the
inspiration of the power of Kosmic Thought that
Life is differentiated into its diverse aspects and
manifestations. All life, that is all individual life
is Created in Kosmos, and by Kosmos, and it is
there that all life is made manifest. It is therefore the source and the manifestation of Life.
Kosmos is able to do this, because all seeds that
are drawn into it, are made through it to conceive
form, and all forms are being indrawn into it and
there renewed. This is through the dual operation
of the processes of creation and dissolution, and
these two are made to act as one harmonious operation. But remember this, its creation is through
conception. When you have mastered this secret,
that is, the secret of Kosmos, you have mastered
the secret of the Great Work. The mystery is that
of conception working in conjunction with dissolution, joined with the ability to draw within all
that is to be either conceived or dissolved. Kosmos
is the great Alchemist, and when any one has
mastered her secret he has himself mastered the
secret of transmutation. When this has been
mastered, the practical work of Alchemy is mere
woman's work and boy's play.

LESSON IX

The Function of the Cosmos

7. Now bodies matter [-made] are in diversity. Some are of the earth, of water some, some are of air, and some of fire.

But they are all composed, some are more [composite], and some are simpler. The heavier ones are more [composed], the lighter less so.

It is the speed of Cosmos' Course that works the manifoldness of the kinds of births. For being a most swift Breath, it doth bestow their qualities on bodies together with the One Pleroma—that of Life.

Now bodies matter [-made] are in diversity. Some are of the earth, of water some, some are of air, and some of fire.

All bodies made from matter may be divided into four classes. They are either formed of earth, of water, of air, or of fire. Thus we have the four groups of bodies, earthy, watery, airy, and fiery bodies. This may be taken as being true in three different senses. In the first place we have the literal application of the classification. At the same time there is the sense in which these terms are used with reference to the four elemental gases, or, rather to the four ethers, that stand back of those gases and manifest through them. Then there is the symbolic sense, in which the four elements are used with reference to their corresponding principles in nature. However, in the main, fire stands for the Hot Principle, air for the Dry Prin-

119

ciple, Water for the Moist Nature, and earth for
the Cold Nature, no matter in what Principle of
nature they may be found. All matter manifests
under those four classifications, and all bodies
made from matter are to be grouped accordingly,
as being fiery, or hot, airy, or dry, watery, or moist,
and earthy, or cold.

But they are all composed; some are more
[composite], and some are simpler. The
heavier ones are more [composed], the
lighter less so.

However, we must not make the mistake of
assuming that there are simple bodies, that is,
bodies formed of a single element. All bodies are
composed of two or more elements. Whichever
element is in the major position in the degree of
composition will determine the element to which
the body belongs. There are in the composition
of these bodies all possible degrees of composition,
from the most composite to the simplest. The
weight of a body depends upon the degree of its
composition, the more it is composed of the different elements, the heavier it becomes, while the
greater the degree of preponderance of a single
element in its composition, the lighter it will be.
This is due to the fact that as the elements are
brought into a closer degree of equilibrium in its
composition, there mutual attraction is increased,
so that the degree of chemical affinity is relatively
increased, and in this way is there an increase in
the attraction which the earth has upon such a
body. Thus it is that the weight of all bodies is
increased in proportion to the degree of their composition. It takes the union of the elements to
form any material body, no matter how small.
Bodies are formed by reason of the combination
of the four elements. Yet the preponderating ele-

ment determines the nature of the body, that is the element which gives to it its nature. Thus we are able to see how all bodies are formed. The elements of chemistry are all composed of these four elements of Alchemy and derive their nature from the proportion in which the four elements unite in their composition. The Molecule is in reality a material body composed of the four elements in diverse proportions, and the same is true of the Atoms of Chemistry. Each one, which is in the nature of the unit of the particular element under consideration, is a material body composed of the four elements. The proportion in which these elements are united in its composition, determines the chemical element to which it will belong. We do not here refer to the atoms of the four elementaries, Oxygen, Hydrogen, Nitrogen and Carbon, but to the eighty-six elements of chemistry. Now, when we bear in mind that all the elements of chemistry are composed of atoms, each of which is composed of the atoms of the four elements of Alchemy, united in a definite proportion, and this in accordance with a perfect mathematical scale, we see the key to the transmutation of these elements the one into the other. All that is necessary is to break up this composition, restoring the chemical element, back into the four elements of Alchemy, and breaking up this order of composition, in such a manner as to change the mathematical proportion of these four elements, until it becomes identical with that of the element to which you wish to change it. Then when you have arranged the proportion exactly right, compose your chemical atom in this way and you have the chemical element which you desire. Unite these atoms into molecules, and you have the physical element which you desire. That is the entire Science and Art of Practical Alchemy. There is nothing to prevent any competent Electro-chemist who has an understanding of the technical side of Analytical Chemistry from transmuting one element into another. We have indicated every problem that is at all involved in the undertaking.

It is the speed of Cosmos' Course that works the manifoldness of the kinds of births. For being a most swift Breath, it doth bestow their qualities on bodies together with the One Pleroma—that of Life.

The Course of Kosmos is in the nature of a most swift Breath. It is a force following an inbreathing and an outbreathing movement; that is, we have the alteration of a Centripetal and a Centrifugal force, and this in perpetuity of action. This movement, not only characterizes, and gives its nature to the one Life, as a simple principle, but it also causes an infinite differentiation in the rapidity of movement in the diverse portion of the four elements. In this way are the diverse qualities engendered. Thus are bodies organized in which are being manifested all of these diverse qualities. In this way are diverse bodies born, in which all the diverse qualities engendered by the course of Kosmic movement, may become incarnate. The One Life which is the Pleroma of all the manifestations of Kosmos, being engendered and made what it is by the movements of the Kosmic Breath, manifests itself through the medium of all the diverse bodies engendered by the swiftness of the Kosmic Breath. In this way, are all bodies made to live, by reason of the Life manifesting through them. Thus in Kosmic motion have we the origin of all modes as well as of Life, and livingness.

8. God, then, is Sire of Cosmos; Cosmos, of [all] in Cosmos. And Cosmos is God's

Son; but things in Cosmos are by Cosmos.

And properly hath it been called Cosmos [Order]; for that it orders all with their diversity of birth, with its not leaving aught without its life, with its unweariedness of activity, the speed of its necessity, the composition of its elements, and order of its ceatures.

The same, then, of necessity and propriety should have the name of Order.

The sense-and-thought, then, of all lives doth come into them from without, inbreathed by what contains [them all]; whereas Cosmos receives them once for all together with its coming into being, and keeps them as a gift from God.

God, then, is Sire of Cosmos; Cosmos, of [all] in Cosmos. And Cosmos is God's Son; but things in Cosmos are by Cosmos.

God is the Sire and source of Kosmos, while all the things in Cosmos are the products of Kosmos. It would therefore be wrong to say that God is the direct creator of anything else save Kosmos. Kosmos is the manifestation of God, while all things in Kosmos are engendered by reason of the life of Kosmos, and hence their being is derived from Kosmos, and they continue to be as a result of the action of Kosmos. They are not of divine origin then, but of kosmic origin. This distinction must at all times be borne in mind, otherwise our thinking will become confused. Kosmos is the womb, projected forth from God, into which all the kosmic seed are deposited and in this way is the kosmic womb fecundated and, as a result it gives birth to all the things in Kosmos. Kosmos is, therefore, in the nature of a self-fecundating womb, which of its own self, fecundates its own self, and out of itself gives birth to all things. It is in the highest sense the Vase of Art, and the fecund womb of existence.

And properly hath it been called Cosmos [Order]; for that it orders all with their diversity of birth, with its not leaving aught without its life, with the unweariedness of its activity, the speed of its necessity, the composition of its elements, and order of its creatures.

Kosmos is in the nature of a vast expanse of energy and substance, every part of its space being equally occupied by both energy and substance. To be a little more explicit we might say that it is a vast space, completely filled with substance, and this substance being completely permeated by dynamic energy. The unweariedness of this activity keeps every particle of this kosmic substance in a state of perpetual motion, thus tending to engender form. This activity engenders a tremendous rate of speed, which, owing to its intense rapidity, manifests a state of necessity, which governs all the other manifestations of Kosmos. All its actions must conform to this necessity. This operation of its necessity results in the composition of all the kosmic elements. A composition, the direct result of the course of kosmic necessity. This course of kosmic necessity, acting upon the kosmic elements, organizes out of them, the diverse forms, and in this way does it order forth the diversity of births of all things in Kosmos. It also infuses the proper quality of life in each thing born, and orders all of its creatures in the true course of evolution through which they are destined to pass in the manifestation of their life. For these reasons is this realm of action, formation, vitalization, composition, necessity, and ordering, termed Kosmos, or Order, for it is the ordering sphere of all things, the-that-which gives order in all things, and having no other source of Order apart from itself.

The same, then, of necessity and of propriety should have the name of **Order.**

Because it is the action of Kosmos that orders forth all things, and assigns to them, the order in which they are made to manifest, it is both necessary and proper that we should give it the name of Order, that which is the cause of the order in which every thing manifests, there being no element of ordering which is not in it, must of necessity be the true foundation of Order, and hence is properly called Order. In other words, it is the principle of Order, and hence is termed Order in the sense of its being the essence of Order, or Order as a Universal Principle.

The sense-and-thought, then, of all lives doth come into them from without, inbreathed by what contains [them all]; whereas Cosmos receives them once for all together with its coming into being, and keeps them as a gift from God.

Sense-and-thought are inherent in no living thing. In all living things sense-and-thought comes into them from without. It is not in any sense of the word a product of any living thing, but emanates from without them all. As it is not in any living thing, it must be inbreathed into them by

some force which is not a thing, and this will have
to be a principle containing within itself all living
things. This can be nothing other than the Kosmos
which we have investigated above. Hence it follows that both sense and thought are inherently and
universally present in Kosmos. In a word, in addi-
tion to forming the body, and infusing it with life
so as to make it live, Kosmos also breathes into it
both sense and thought, which makes it instinctive
and intelligent. This is all the work of Kosmos.
It will be perfectly correct if we say that we live
in Kosmos at all times, completely immersed in it,
and completely bathed in the Kosmic sea. We are
breathing in, life, sense, and thought from Kosmos
as well as air from the Atmosphere. But more
properly will it be to say that these are being
breathed into us by Kosmos, for we are the Negative side and not the Positive side of this relationship. Kosmos, in its coming into being, receives
sense-and-thought as an integral part of its being.
They remain inseparably united with its being,
for were it not for Kosmic Sense and Kosmic
Thought, Kosmos would not be Kosmos. This will
at once appear, when we bear in mind that the
nature of Kosmos is the Ultimate Order. Now,
this Order is maintained through the operation of
sense-and-thought, and hence, Kosmos depends
upon the perpetual presence of this kosmic sense-
and-thought. Man senses that which already is,
and through his sensing, he comes in contact with
it, but Kosmos senses that which does not exist,
and through such sensing of the non-existent, it is
brought into existence through the action of the
kosmic sense. The action of sense-and-thought are
exactly the reverse in the case of man, and of Kosmos. Man senses that which is exterior to himself
and this sensing of the object causes him to think
of it, so that thought springs out of his sensing. In
the case of Kosmos, however, thought precedes

sense. Through sense, the thing thought of is brought into existence. Through Kosmic sense, the kosmic thoughts are made sensible, and in this way they begin to exist. Kosmic sense is therefore the kosmic faculty of rendering the subjective thought side of Kosmos, objective. When man has transformed this human sense into kosmic sense, he has acquired the power of making his subjective thought objective, that is of objectifying his thought images, and thus of creating that which he thinks in his mind. This is the true secret of creation. When one has mastered this secret he is the master of the Art of Creation, and thus has he attained creative thought through the mastering of kosmic sense. Kosmic sense-and-thought are the reflection in kosmic substance of the sense-and-thought of God. It is in this sense that the sense-and-thought of Kosmos is a gift from God, it is the sense-and-thought of God manifesting through Kosmic Substance. The sense-and-thought of man are in turn, the manifestation of the kosmic sense-and-thought through the medium of the human organism. For this reason we might truly say, the sense-and-thought of man is a gift from Kosmos. It is this connection which enables man to rise from the status of the human man to that of the kosmic man, through the incarnation in himself, of kosmic sense and kosmic thought. Such transposition of himself and of his powers to the kosmic status is the true secret as well as the true goal of the Alchemist, and this is the *Ultama thule* of the Hermetic Art. This is the great distinction between the Natural and the Artistic Man. The great problem is to open up oneself to the activities of the Kosmos, and permit them a freer degree of manifestation through our diverse principles. To ensoul as far as we are able, Kosmos, is the Magnum Opus in all of its completeness.

LESSON X

The Sense-and-Thought of God

9. But God is not, as some suppose, beyond the reach of sense-and-thought. It is through superstition men thus impiously speak.

For all the things that are, Asclepius, all are in God, are brought by God to be, and do depend on Him—both things that act through bodies, and things that through soul-substance make [other things] to move, and things that make things live by means of spirit, and things that take unto themselves the things that are worn out.

And rightly so; nay, I would rather say, He doth not *have* these things; but I speak forth the truth, He *is* them all Himself. He doth not *get* them from without, but *gives* them out [from Himself].

This is God's sense-and-thought, even to move all things. And never time shall be when e'en a whit of things that are shall cease; and when I say "a whit of things that are," I mean a whit of God. For things that are, God hath; nor aught [is there] without Him, nor [is] He without aught.

But God is not, as some suppose, beyond the reach of sense-and-thought. It is through superstition men thus impiously speak.

Those who assume that God is absolutely transcendent and cannot be approached, are the ignorant and the superstitious. The whole theory of the transcendence of God is entirely due to a misunderstanding of the nature of God. The principle reason for such contention is that it renders it impossible for man to know God and His Will, and this renders a Revelation of God necessary. Thus we have the belief that we can only reach a knowledge of God through revelation, and of course this is a very convenient doctrine for the clergy, as it makes them the sole custodians of the Will of God. I might say that this idea of a transcendent God, the knowledge of Whom comes only by revelation, is the deliberate invention of the priesthood, and it is one of the most useful of all inventions, for it is of course at all times essential that we should befuddle the cheap organisms, and in this way it will be the easier for us to exploit them. It is impious for anyone to say that God cannot be reached through sense-and-thought. As a matter of fact, the sense-and-thought of man is quite capable of at-oneing itself with God, so that simply through his sense-and-thought man may know God definitely and with complete satisfaction. This of course is not the privilege of cheap organisms, only gentlemen have any business to know God!

For all the things that are, Asclepius, all are in God, are brought by God to be, and do depend on Him—both things that act through bodies, and things that through soul-substance make [other things] to move, and things that make things live by means of spirit, and things that take unto themselves the things that are worn out.

Nothing ever comes into being unless it was previously in God. That is, things come into existence because they have previously subsisted in God. Not only is this true, but they continue to subsist in Him after they have been born into existence. In fact, the only cause for the existence of anything is the abiding idea of it in God. They are in God, they are brought by Him into being, and their continued existence depends upon Him. They can exist only so long as He is conscious of them as being in Him. This will mean that they can exist only because they subsist in His consciousness. They have no other substratum than God. He does not create them, He externalizes them from the depths of Himself alone. In a word, all things are generated in Ku, are born forth out of Ku, and at the same time ever continue to abide in Ku. This is true of everything that lives and acts through the instrumentality of a body, that is, all embodied life. In a word, every single body that exists, subsists in God, has been born forth out of God, and depends for its continued existence upon the continued presence in God of its arche-typal idea. But this is not only true of all embodied things, but it is true as well of those motive forces that manifest through soul-substance and in this way move other things. In a word, every form of dynamic energy subsists in God, has been emanated from God and depends for its continued activity upon the fact that it is still in God. Also, all those things that are the causes of the infusing of spirit into other things, and in this way make them to live, are likewise in God, they have been manifested out from God, and at the same time they continue to subsist in God. Likewise, those things that devour or absorb the things that have lived out their period of life, and are hence worn out, are also subsistent in God, are existent from God and continue to depend upon

God for their being. In a word, every single thing
in the Kosmos, in the Universe, in the earth, and
everywhere else, has subsisted in God, it has been
born forth from God into existence, and it continues to abide in God as to its ideal form. Therefore, we see that God is all-in-all. That all things
are but aspects of His being, made active, and in
this way made manifest. Hence there is nothing
apart from Him. Not only have all things been
brought into being through the act of God, but
likewise, they continue to exist only because of the
continual sustenance of God to them, they are His
perpetual manifestations.

And rightly so; nay, I would rather say,
He doth not *have* these things; but I speak
forth the truth, He *is* them all Himself. He
doth not *get* them from without, but *gives*
them out [from Him].

God has not created these things. They are not
His creatures, neither does He have them as
possessions. In no sense are they to be separated
from Him. They are not to be thought of as His
works, neither should we in truth speak of them
as emanations from Him. In reality, God is all
these things Himself. He does not get these things
from some other source. They are not derived from
another, neither do they come from outside of God.
On the other hand, God gives them all out from
Himself. In a word, all things are born forth
from God. Now, if they are born of Him, they
must have been formed previously to the time of
such birth, and if they are born of God, they can
be formed of nothing apart from Him, hence they
must have been formed in God. If they are formed
in Him, they can be formed of nothing which is
not present in Him at a time previous to such
forming, hence, they will of necessity have to be

formed of the substance of God Himself. In a word, they will have to be formed of Ku and in Ku. As all the divine formations take place in Ku and as a result of thought, it will follow that God must first think of the thing to be formed; that is, he must think the thought corresponding to the thing that is going to be formed, for, bear in mind God does not intend to form this or that, His thought, on the contrary, engenders that which corresponds to it. The Divine Thought impregnates Ku, and as a result that which corresponds to the thought is formed in the womb of Ku. From this it will follow that it must be formed of the substance of Ku and energized by Her energy, thus it will be quite divine. All things are therefore the thoughts of God, manifesting through the substance and energy of God. There is no other thought, no other substance, and no other energy save that of God, hence, all things are of this thought, substance and energy of God and have nothing else, hence, they are all of them, God. Therefore, God is each and every thing of all things that are. He is not only all things, but He is each particular thing. To be a little more explicit, no thing has any objective existence. They all have an existence purely subjective, subsisting in the consciousness of God, but do not exist as objects. It is illusion that causes us to see them as objective; they are in fact thoughts of God, existing merely as states of His sense. In no other sense do they exist. Hence, they are to all intents and purposes God Himself.

This is God's sense-and-thought, ever to move all things. And never time shall be when e'en a whit of things that are shall cease; and when I say "a whit of things that are," I mean a whit of God. For things that are, God hath, nor aught [is there] without Him, nor [is] He without aught.

The sense-and-thought of God is the power that moves all things. They are engendered by His thought, and after they have been engendered, that thought abides in them, thus becoming their intelligence, and in this way, directing from within, all their movements. The sense of God is that which causes them to have form, for they are in form, because they are in the sense of God, and for no other reason. Were they to cease to be sensible to Him they would cease to be. Energy they have because of the sense of God, for His energy is His sense. Therefore, all things are brought into being and are made to move, through the sense of God. It is in fact the sense of God abiding in all things that causes them to move by reason of the movement which is within them, this is true because all things are ensouled by the sense of God. The time can never come when a whit of things that are shall cease to be, because, all such things have merely a subjective existence in the thought and sense of God, hence they can never cease to be, so long as God is sensible of them. Until such time as God shall become insensible of His own thought-and-sense, nothing existing in His thought-and-sense can ever cease to be. As His thought-and-sense are His Being, it follows that the very being of God must change before any thing can ever cease to be, and owing to the immutability of His Essence this is impossible. All things are therefore so many parts of God, and as no part of God can be destroyed, seeing that He is not composed, but is the Absolute Unity, the dissolution of any part of Him would be the extinction of His unity, it follows that nothing that has come into being, can ever cease to be. There is nothing without God, hence nothing has existence save as God.

This being the case, God does not subsist, save as the totality of the all, hence God cannot survive if any single thing is lost. This soul-satisfying Omni-Theism solves all the problems of existence and subsistence. We can see that there are no things, but on the contrary, there is the Absolute One whose relativity appears to be diverse.

10. These things should seem to thee, Asclepius, if thou dost understand them, true; but if thou dost not understand, things not to be believed.

To understand is to believe, to not believe is not to understand.

My word (*logos*) doth go before [thee] to the truth. But mighty is the mind, and when it hath been led by word up to a certain point, it hath the power to come before thee to the truth.

And having thought o'er all these things, and found them consonant with those which have already been translated by the reason, it hath [e'en] now believed, and found its rest in that Fair Faith.

To those, then, who by God ['s good aid] do understand the things that have been said [by us] above, they're credible; but unto those who understand them not, incredible.

Let so much, then, suffice on thought-and-sense.

These things should seem to thee, Asclepius, if thou dost understand them, true; but if thou dost not undrestand, things not to be believed.

The teaching that we have been giving here on the subject of thought-and-sense, will at once appear to be the truth, if one understands the true meaning of what has been said. If one is able to comprehend our interpretation, he will at once see that it could not possibly have been any other way. To one who understands our meaning, the truth of what we have said will be self-evident. If this is not the case, it will simply prove that the unbeliever has simply no comprehension whatsoever of what we are talking about. In a word, it will go to show, that he is not capable of forming an opinion on such subjects, in a word, it will expose him as a cheap organism. The beauty of the Hermetic position is in the fact that once it has been understood, an intelligent person cannot possibly see how it would be possible for it to be any other way.

To understand is to believe, to not believe is not to understand.

Here we have a definition of belief that may strike many as being unusual. Belief, is in reality that action of the mind by which a statement is accepted as being true. There is no connection between true belief and credulity. It is impossible for any one to believe that which he does not understand, and likewise, it is impossible for one to avoid belief in that which he understands. The function of the understanding is to trace out the relationship between a statement and the synthesis of truth of which one is conscious. To understand a statement is therefore, to trace out the relationship which that statement bears to the truth of which one is aware. When the mind has indicated this relationship, and has shown that there is no point at which the relationship is not perfect, one has understood the statement. Belief is that action

of the mind, by which, when a statement is understood, it is registered as being true. In a word,
that which we believe we accept as being real,
while up to the point of belief, it was merely
apparent. It might be true, or it might not. However, belief is the act of mind by which that which
is understood becomes certain. We are sure of
what we believe. One never believes any thing on
the testimony of another. The testimony of others
may establish a presumption in favor of a statement of fact, but it is not sufficient to establish a
belief. We do not believe a thing until the understanding has indicated why it is true. In a word,
to believe is to accept the connection between the
fact and the Law of Nature that is operative in
the establishing of that fact. We will go a step
farther, it is not at all easy to believe any thing
that is not true. Belief as we have indicated is
a condition of mind resulting from an understanding of the thing to be believed, and is in all cases,
a condition subsequent to the understanding of the
proposition. To accept a statement on the authority of another, is not to believe it, but to admit that
the other has a mind superior to your own, and
therefore, what he says must be true, but you can
never realize that it is true, and that is what you
have to do if you are to believe it. This certitude
of belief is the result of the understanding of the
statement.

My word (*logos*) doth go before [thee]
to the truth. But mighty is the mind, and
when it hath been led by word up to a certain
point, it hath the power to come before
[thee] to the truth.

When the truth is taught in the form of words,
it will give a statement of the truth, which one

cannot at the moment accept as the truth. In other words, one can have stated to him in the form of words, a truth which he does not as yet understand as such. The purpose of such teaching is to set the mind at work, and directing it along a certain line of thought, cause it, through this process, to formulate the concept, in terms of thought ere we are conscious of the fact that we have accepted it as being true. In a word, man never believes a statement because he wishes to believe it, he believes it because the belief is made manifest in his mind. In other words, we are dealing with a form of chemical action, and the act of listening to the teaching has the effect of confining the action of the mind to the topic under discussion, with the result that the understanding works it out, and the result is, the germination in the mind of a definite belief in that which has been brought to its attention. This is in fact pure alchemy. It is also true that we reach such belief at a time anterior to our becoming conscious of the fact that we have accepted it as being true. We must at all times bear in mind that all mental operations are in the nature of achievements in Alchemy. For this reason, the purpose of instruction is nothing more than the discipline of the mind, to the end that its operations may be confined to a certain line of thought, and in this way belief may be born within it. You can prove nothing to any one, you can merely lead his mind in the right direction, so that it may of its own power, create within itself the belief of the thing which you wish to impress upon it.

And having thought o'er all these things, and found them consonant with those which have already been translated by the reason, it hath [e'en now] believed, and found its rest in that Fair Faith.

The function of the reason is to translate all things into the form of belief. It is closely connected with the understanding, and yet there is a distinction. The great work of reason is to analyze all statements and reducing them to their most ultimate aspect, to detect errors. It is in fact the critical faculty. By it we are able to detect any defects that may be present in its presentation. It is in fact, the Dweller on the Threshold which every statement must pass before it can approach the understanding. Through the exercise of the reason, all statements of views, are analyzed and are at last reduced to such form as will accommodate them to the body of truth. They are then, being translated into this form, given to the understanding, which assimulates them in such way that we have an understanding of them, when they take the form of belief. It is therefore the reason that translates all things into the form of belief. When all these things which we are here discussing have been carefully thought over, and as a result of such thinking, have been found to be consonant with those which have already been translated by the reason, in other words, thinking on them, so that the reason has prepared them for assimilation into the understanding, so that they may become a part of what has been accepted as belief, the mind believes in them. This will simply mean that the mind has made of them a portion of its own belief. They will have taken their abode in the mind, so that from this time forth, all one's thinking will be conditioned by these things. This is an operation of pure Alchemy which transpires in the mind. Words have been transmuted into beliefs. It is thus that one believes the Gnosis. Thus through such belief of the teaching, one takes his rest in the Fair Faith of Gnosis. The Fair Faith is in no sense to be confused with what is com-

monly called blind faith. To find rest in the Fair
Faith means that through thinking upon the
Gnostic Teaching, the reason is to translate it in
terms of one's individual understanding, and thus
it is to engender belief of the Gnosis. This belief
in the Gnostic Teaching will so transform the
mind that in all of its future thinking, it will operate in that direction and in accordance with those
principles, and that transformed state of mind is
Gnosis, or it is the Fair Faith. This then is not in
the nature of a belief, but rather in the nature of
a state of mind, that will transform into its likeness all the things that are offered to the mind.
This is in fact the Golden Mind which will transform into its own Pure Gold all the baser thoughts
that are born within it. Gnosis is therefore the
Philosopher's Stone, that is to transform into
Gnosis all the thoughts of the mind. After one
has taken his rest in this Fair Faith, it is utterly
impossible for him to ever err, for the reason that
his Faith will make all his thinking after its image.

To those, then, who by God ['s good aid]
do understand the things that have been said
[by us] above, they're credible; but unto
those who understand them not, incredible.

If one has understood this teaching, it means that
his reason has translated it into terms of his thinking, and that his understanding has united it with
his previous knowledge, so that it has through the
action of his mind become a belief, and hence a
part of his thinking. This being true, it will follow that they are real to him, being part and parcel
of his mental organization and hence of his thinking. This being the case, it is quite impossible for
him to doubt them any longer. On the other hand,
if one has not understood them, they are no part of

his mind, and as he does not think them, of course
he cannot believe them, seeing that no such belief
has been born within his mind. One repudiates
these things, simply because of the fact that no such
belief has been born within the mind, and in the
absence of such a belief, it is futile for us to expect
one to accept them. One who accepts the Gnosis
is merely one who has consummated the Great
Work in his mind, while one who has not consummated it will of course be unable to accept a belief
which can only exist as a result of such consummation of the Great Work in the mind. Faith in
Gnosis is born within the mind, and it comes in no
other way. Unless this has been born in the mind,
it is useless to hope for one to see the truth in our
sublime teaching. This bearing of the Fair Faith
in the mind is the true purpose of the Hermetic
Art. All Hermetic Disciplines lead unto this end.

Let so much, then, suffice on thought-and-
sense.

What we have said in the above instructions will
clearly indicate the exact nature of thought-and-
sense, divine, kosmic and human. Those who will
not understand our interpretation are cheap organisms that would not understand were we to write
ten thousand volumes on the subject, and to those
capable of understanding, we have given ample
instruction for their guidance in the working of
the Hermetic Art and the consummation of the
Great Work in their own minds. This is the
Master Key to the transmutation of the mind and
the generation of thought, belief and Faith. We
have indicated the one and only way in which one
ever attains Gnosis. Remember this, you can never
learn Gnosis, it is useless to study it. Gnosis must
be born within you, and it can be born only in the

mind, and that in the way that we have here indicated. The attainment of Gnosis is the Magnum
Opus of the mind.

With these words, we close our treatise on The
Hermetic Art. Those who have understood us,
will have no difficulty in going into the study of
the Art of Alchemy.

(The End)

Printed in July 2021
by Rotomail Italia S.p.A., Vignate (MI) - Italy